PENGUIN CANADA

Colin & Justin's Home Heist Style Guide

Colin McAllister and **Justin Ryan** are the resident designers and hosts of HGTV Canada's hit show *Colin & Justin's Home Heist*. They have hosted several TV shows around the world, including *Colin & Justin's How Not to Decorate, Trading Up,* and *Colin & Justin's Home Show,* as well as a BBC Radio program, *Colin & Justin's Music Makeover.* They are also the authors of the internationally bestselling books *The Million Pound Property Experiment* and *How Not to Decorate,* and have written for several publications in Canada and the United Kingdom, including *Canadian Style at Home, Metro, Driven, Sharp,* the *National Post, The Sunday Mail,* and *The Sunday Mirror.*

Also by Colin & Justin

How Not to Decorate
The Million Pound Property Experiment

HOME HEIST
STYLE GUIDE
How to Create the Perfect Home

Colin McAllister & Justin Ryan

PENGUIN
CANADA

PENGUIN CANADA

Published by the Penguin Group

Penguin Group (Canada), 90 Eglinton Avenue East, Suite 700, Toronto, Ontario, Canada
M4P 2Y3 (a division of Pearson Canada Inc.)

Penguin Group (USA) Inc., 375 Hudson Street, New York, New York 10014, U.S.A.
Penguin Books Ltd, 80 Strand, London WC2R 0RL, England
Penguin Ireland, 25 St Stephen's Green, Dublin 2, Ireland (a division of Penguin Books Ltd)
Penguin Group (Australia), 250 Camberwell Road, Camberwell, Victoria 3124, Australia (a division of Pearson Australia Group Pty Ltd)
Penguin Books India Pvt Ltd, 11 Community Centre, Panchsheel Park, New Delhi – 110 017, India
Penguin Group (NZ), 67 Apollo Drive, Rosedale, North Shore 0745, Auckland, New Zealand (a division of Pearson New Zealand Ltd)
Penguin Books (South Africa) (Pty) Ltd, 24 Sturdee Avenue, Rosebank, Johannesburg 2196, South Africa

Penguin Books Ltd, Registered Offices: 80 Strand, London WC2R 0RL, England

First published 2008

1 2 3 4 5 6 7 8 9 10

ISBN 978-0-14-317057-0

Library and Archives Canada Cataloguing in Publication data available upon request to the publisher

Visit the Penguin Group (Canada) website at **www.penguin.ca**

Special and corporate bulk purchase rates available; please see **www.penguin.ca/corporatesales** or call 1-800-810-3104, ext. 477 or 474

HOME HEIST
STYLE GUIDE
How to Create the Perfect Home

Contents

Acknowledgments

This book is dedicated to the memory of two great men: our beloved fathers, Robert McAllister and Daniel Ryan, whom we miss every day. We wish you could have been here to see how much we love our new Canadian chapter.

And to our Mums, Claire Ryan and Trudy McAllister, both of whom keep the home fires burning. Scotland is all the better for your presence.

To our team at Penguin Canada (Tracy Bordian, Helen Reeves, Alina Goldstein, Mary Opper, Kerrin Hands, and Wendy Thomas), whose unstinting dedication has allowed us to create this literary and visual feast! We remain forever in your debt. Thank you for your patience and for believing in this wonderful project from day one. We are SO proud of this book.

A huge thank you to the wonderful Anna Gecan at HGTV, without whose guidance and support our crazy Canadian journey might never have happened. Thank you for persuading us to take a giant leap of faith … all the way across the Atlantic! Thanks also to Michelle Kosoy, Tanya Linton, and Karen Gelbert for belief in our brand. To Jen Knox, Muriel Solomon, Caroline Lennox, and Ursula Terlecki for pushing press boundaries beyond our wildest expectation. And to Munro, Sam, and Stephen for utterly inspired marketing strategies.

To our directors Danielle Kiraly and Cheryl Zalameda (and their associates Meagan, Missy, Karen, Julie, and Val) for creative storytelling prowess and glorious *Home Heist* belief through crazy times. Thank you for *everything*.

To Dave, Tim, Dustin, Ben, Jaques O, Steve, Graeme, Greg, Matt, and Brian, who (literally) built our designer dreams.

To Colin, Gee, and all our camera op.'s and audio boys for capturing everything with such visual perfection. And to our favourite sound man Chris (Bunting) Davies for making it all sound so wonderful! To Ken, our camera assistant, for genius comic timing. And to genius post-production teams (on both sides of the Atlantic) for allowing the *Home Heist* message to travel to more than twenty countries.

To our awesome art director Laura Fowler, who, as far as we're concerned, is God. And a proper LADY into the designer bargain! Sufficient words don't exist to explain how we feel about you. Thank you from here to artistic eternity and back.

For Cheryl Torrenueva, our design manager (and beautiful on-screen Angel), without whose loyalty and passion we would have struggled to create this degree of decorative majesty. Never leave us—PLEASE! We love you like our little sister. But just one thing … no more flat shoes!

To the rest of our wonderful art department—Felice, Susie, Aiden, Jean, and Katherine—to name but a few—as well as all our devoted interns, who so perfectly interpret our designer dreams. Our world is a better place for working with you.

To our producers, Amy Hoskings, Ife Okwudili, and Gloria Wood. To Philip Whelan, Nick Cory Wright, Rob Carey, Simon and Jane Lloyd, Pixie Black, and Suzie Choueri, as well as the entire team at Nextfilm.

To Scott and Stephen, our drivers, and to the wonderful Steve Hart. And to our beautiful make-up artist, Katie Solomon, without whose endless effervesence we might have wilted. Even on dark days you bring us to life. And you know we love you, huh?

To Sue Knight, our British agent, and Alison Griffin, our British publicist, for loyally nurturing our opportunity during the last decade.

To the wondrous Martha Watson, our Canadian publicist and literary agent, who brokered this fabulous Penguin book. There has not been one moment in your company we haven't enjoyed. Friends, forever!

To Peter, Debs, and Fhiona in Glasgow—we miss you every day. Thanks for remembering us while we're across The Pond. And to Cherri and David, our lovely new Canadian friends. Thank God for that chance meeting at Cirque de Soleil…

To Winston and Felix, our heavenly feline angels. You'd have so loved our sunny Canadian terrace. Our world is emptier without you, boys.

To Michaela Davies for true altruism and outstanding generosity. Your heart is the size of Canada.

To Shalini, Tina, and all at DMG, and to Marilyn Denis for finding space on her sofa each time we had something to talk about! And to Beelze'Bob Lawlor and his wonderful boys for endless parties and access into their gang.

And to Scotland—for allowing us the opportunity to run off for a wee while and explore pastures new. You KNOW we will always come home. And to Canada—for allowing us into your fabulous world. "We stand on guard for thee…"

To all the folk we've "heisted"—your homes provide a stage for our creativity. Thank you.

And, finally, to our fans on both sides of the Atlantic. Your support has been mind-blowing. Thank you for reading and thank you for watching. We hope you enjoy this book!

Colin McAllister and Justin Ryan

Finding Your Style

CANADIAN HOMEOWNERS ARE INCREDIBLY fortunate—many have spacious, modern abodes, and others live in smaller, older houses. But most homeowners we've worked with have one problem: They simply don't know who they are when it comes to style. Sure, many people have a disconnected idea of what they do and don't like, but somehow the struggle to create that perfect home continues.

Think about this scenario: You're at the mall shopping for home items and you simply can't decide what you're looking for. You wander aimlessly searching for things—*any* things! Every now and then something catches your eye and, though it may not be *exactly* what you're looking for, you think, "Oh what the hell—I'm tired, I'm bored, and I have to buy *something!*" Of course what happens next is classic; you get the item home, it does *nothing* for your room, and you either put up with it or you take it back to the store. The way we see it, bad design comes from bad planning, which leads, in turn, to bad shopping. Learn to think about what you want well in advance and then let your lifestyle dictate your home style. Base your buying decisions on how you use each space, the architectural period of your home, and the particular style to which you tend to be drawn. It really is important to pin down *who* you are, *what*, precisely, you want from your home, and

how exactly you plan to achieve it. Which, in short, means no more impulse buys!

To properly discover who you are—and what you really like—first pore over every home interest magazine you can find and assemble a pile of tear-outs of the things you like. Watch all the home interest television you can (paying particular attention to our shows!) and take note of the things that excite you. Now, consider the period of your house and put together a mental Identikit of all the elements you'd like it to include, drawing on your research. With any luck you should start to see an identity emerging. This is simply the start of discovering who you are at home …

As soon as you become familiar with the basic styles of interior decorating, you'll begin to have a better grasp of how to define your own style and you'll begin to understand the rules of design. But of course like *any* rules, these rules can (sometimes) be broken. Careful scrutiny of style and home fashion should eventually give you the confidence to buck trends, try out new colours, and start mixing moods to create individual identity. Which is the next step to discovering who you are at home …

Home styles can be grouped into the following categories:

Traditional: This direction uses decorated furnishings, lavish rich fabrics, and dark woods such as cherry and mahogany. It's normally quite a formal style but we like to loosen it up a little by adding unexpected modern or more casual touches.

Country: Ah, gorgeous! A simple and friendly look that features lots of painted wood (even ex-knotty pine!) mixed with antiques and collectibles to create a cozy warm atmosphere.

Coastal: Inspired by the beach and all things pertaining to the sea. This look is traditionally clean and cool. It mixes a myriad of blue with stone—as well as sandy—shades and, depending on your furnishings and home build style, it can be either traditional or contemporary and will appeal to most age groups.

Contemporary: Spacious with clean lines, lots of natural light, acres of glass, and interesting architecturally shaped furniture. Contemporary "soft minimalism" works for many, and the mood is generally dramatic in a pared-down technological way.

Romantic: Rich damask prints, soft linens, and aged furnishings create a look that is very elegant. This look can be slightly girly if it's assembled with pink and lace but it can be surprisingly masculine if deeper tones such as aubergine or grey are selected.

Natural and Neutral: The colours of the earth—stone, green, and bronze tempered with white and cream—conspire to deliver this particular look. Select blond wood like beech and birch for contemporary Scandinavian-inspired results.

Shabby Chic: Mixing old and new (with the emphasis on old) is the order of the day with this look. Worn around the edges is good news, and furnishings actually benefit from a battered and slightly "time-travelled" look. It must be done carefully, though, or you'll just have plain old shabby.

Global Styles

Pan-Asian: Square-cut, pared-down Japanese minimalism or richly adorned chinoiserie. Furniture is generally sculptural and beautiful and living spaces are zoned according to function.

Santa Fe Style: A decorating style that employs earth tones, terracotta accessories, rich textures, and naïve, simple adornment.

French Provincial: The roots of this scheme lie in metals and deep, matte shades of colour. It's all about lusciously languid daybeds, rich heavy cotton linens, hugely dominating armoires, and just a sprinkling of gold detail.

English Country House: Imagine Buckingham Palace in miniature and you've got the gist. Rich fabrics, patterned Axminster carpets, loads of baby blue, soft green, or palest pink upholstery, as well as striped wallpapers and cream and gold accessory accents. Oh yes, and just a smattering of antiques …

Moroccan Style: This look elicits a rich dark mood. It's influenced by Hispanic and Moorish style. Imagine deep jewel colours, patterned brass, fretwork timber, patterned tiles, and bringing the outside in. Add loads of tapestry, touches of velvet, and shot silk and you're there.

We could go on and on and list a veritable globe of inspiration, but the important thing for you is to discover what's out there—whether through travel, film, TV, magazines, or books—and then use that inspiration to create a beautiful home. It's worth noting, though, that while a room full of bright floor cushions might look great in the Kasbah, it could be horribly impractical in Calgary. Just remember: Let your lifestyle dictate your home style and create design that is relevant to your world.

Practical as Well as Beautiful

Take note of everything you use your home for and let those aspects influence your style choices too. Time to ask yourself more questions! Do you tend to entertain a lot? Casually or formally? Do you aspire to create a quiet retreat or are you a party animal who needs a stage on which to perform? Does the perfect night-in whisper romantic dinner for two, or is your home life more about TV dinners on trays for the entire family? We can only suggest! You are the one with the answers.

Look for the Home Clues to Find Out Who You Are

When designing, we always look at existing style "evidence" in our clients' homes and then base our decisions accordingly. For example, in the first episode of *Home Heist*, our owners had a collection of Buddhas in their hutch (among all the clutter) so we started to see signals that they loved all things Asian. With a direction decided, we created a relevant master bedroom with a lovely Thai-inspired feel.

You should do the same kind of research we did. Become your own personal home "shrink" and analyze the evidence to find commonality:

Repetitive Behaviour: Do you tend to favour one particular colour or do you have a heartfelt passion for, and huge collection of, art deco china? If you've got a blue door, blue carpet, and blue bedroom, chances are you like blue!

Shopping Habits: Do you gravitate toward Pottery Barn or is Minotti more your thing? Does a rummage through your local flea market bring a huge smile to your face? Where and how you source your furnishings tells a lot about who you are and, even if your ideas are influenced by advertising, at least you've got a feel for how you want your home to be!

"Brave" Purchases: Is there one new item of furniture that's *completely* out of synch with the rest of your home? Perhaps this is the first step into a style you as yet don't have the confidence to follow through on.

Favourite Hotel and Holiday Destination: Are cozy English B&Bs your thing or are Manhattan hotel suites and city escapes more desirable? Is barefoot living in hot tropical climes your idea of heaven? Listen to your own style signals and be inspired by your travels to create a look that's right for you. As Belinda Carlisle once said, heaven is a place on earth.

Personal Taste: Choosing art, film, or music is like choosing a partner—we all see what's beautiful and personal to *us*. With this in mind, learn to be inspired by your own taste to create an appropriate home style. If, for example, sci-fi posters and replica ray guns are your idea of decor, then quite possibly a modern, technological home is for you. If art deco prints,

however, are more relevant, then creating a classic look with clean lines is more likely to make you happy.

Learn from Past Triumphs: Did you absolutely adore the living room in your last house, or do you love your current bedroom? Analyze what it is that you love so much and then employ that elusive ingredient across other rooms to create a feeling of personal continuity. If you got it right before, then you can do it again.

Update Your Influences: Once you've got an idea of who you are at home—and how you want your place to look—you should finally be able to create your ideal world. But remember that a perfect home should be an organic and fluid environment. So make sure you keep updating your space to keep it fresh and exciting. You don't have to spend a lot of cash on new furniture every month, but do keep an eye on clutter and anything that looks a bit tired … and attend to it immediately.

In the following pages, we'll expound on these basic ideas as they apply to individual rooms, the furniture, and design principles. We suggest you read the Living Rooms chapter through before starting on the other rooms, as it contains information that's relevant to all room design. But for now … prepare to have your home heisted in true Colin and Justin style!

The

Rooms

Living Rooms

AH, THE LIVING ROOM. THAT WONDERFUL SHARING SPACE THAT WILL, IF YOU GET IT *RIGHT*, become a centre of relaxation for you and everybody you live with. Get it *wrong,* however, and you'll end up never relaxing and in a terrifying space that would rival any of the before shots featured in this book. So be warned!

But panic not, we can show you how to make your living room—be it a monolithic space or a compact wee nook—utterly perfect. From advice about layout and how to select perfect furniture to tips on colour scheming and identifying which look is truly appropriate for your space, we'll guide you through the maze of decorating rights and wrongs. And the best part? Creating the perfect living room is actually a whole load of fun! Before we go any further, however, our first word of advice is ... STOP! Don't rush. Take your time and decide what you expect from your living room. Will it be used every day? And by how many people? How good is the natural light?

Which are you—modernist or traditionalist? What kind of furniture do you like best? Yup, the list goes on and on, and we'll work through the most important issues in the following pages. So stop, take a breath, and allow us to show you how to become decorating *winners* instead of decorating *sinners!*

Finding the Living Room Look that Works Best for You

WE RECKON THAT FROM MILES OFF, WE CAN spot living rooms (and other rooms) that have been put together as fashion statements as opposed to environments that have been carefully assembled to reflect their occupants' true style. And believe us, the former and the latter are two completely different things. A well-planned space shouldn't *scream* "designer," it should gently *whisper* "design." There's little more off-putting than a stilted scene that looks ready-made, off the shelf, or simply too of the moment. One of the first things we do with our clients (whether they're TV contributors or those with whom we work through private commission) is sit them down to figure out what type of room they need. What are their favourite colours, what period of architecture do they most enjoy, what is their favourite restaurant? Do they enjoy travel? And if so, what is their favourite country? It may seem odd to ask questions that aren't related directly to the use of the room, but an information harvest such as this is a tried and tested route we follow to establish likes and dislikes and assemble relevant information to help decide a project's direction.

It all comes down to careful planning to ensure the completed project doesn't appear less than relaxed. If, for example, you like traditional rooms stuffed with antiques, it generally follows that you mightn't feel completely at home in a loft space that screams Wall Street 1985. Even, that is, if Wall Street 1985 is terribly *de rigueur* as far as your fave magazine editors are concerned! Conversely, if you absolutely adore art deco–inspired schemes, filling your home with Victoriana (just because your neighbours have done so and it looks great) isn't going to result in a setting within which you feel comfortable.

So be as honest with yourself as you possibly can. Consider the likes and dislikes of all the people with whom you share your home and then plan accordingly—with them in mind too.

Using Mood Boards

We create room-specific mood boards for *every* project—we find this to be great fun, relatively simple, yet absolutely critical. A mood board is created on a white piece of board. Samples of all relevant materials can be arranged on it to see what works and what doesn't. First we play around with potential fabric and wallpaper samples to see how they work together. Next, we test patterns against paint charts to help imagine our vision and then we mingle different textures and motifs to help us visualize the end result. We tear pages from magazines as visual reminders of all the things that have caught our eye, and we study these pictures to analyze their design relationship with all other aspects of our scheme. It might sound like a lot of effort but we think you'll find it rewarding to do on your own as you contemplate your new design. The best designs are those that are carefully conceived and thoughtfully planned. Believe us—if you cheat and rush in to things, don't expect your project to work in a way that pleases you. As we always say, "To fail to plan … is to plan to fail."

Planning the Perfect Relaxation Space

These days, few homes can boast a living room that is set aside simply for lounging. Most of today's living rooms double as offices or dining rooms and therefore need to be capable of shifting atmospheric gear on a whim. As such, our watchword is *flexibility*. At the flick of a

switch a room that is by day the perfect chill-out zone can change tempo to cope with the imminent arrival of dinner guests.

We have a few easy tricks for achieving this transformation. Don't stop with our examples, though—once you start looking at your space this way, you're bound to come up with creative ideas.

☀ Sometimes the only thing required to introduce intimacy and atmospheric dining is to highlight an existing accent wall. A warm conversation-promoting shade such as red can be suddenly enlivened with a directional spotlight.

☀ Perhaps the only thing that stands between a multi-function family room and a place for Mum and Dad to snuggle up for an evening is a pair of family-friendly sofas that can be pulled together to make a cozy nest in which to watch your favourite HGTV shows! It's worth thinking about all these aspects before buying furniture.

☀ The home office has become a necessity but sometimes it's the corner office—and we don't mean the one where the CEO sits! If your home office has to be part of your living room (or indeed any other room), being able to hide it away quickly is vital. Look for modular furniture or furniture with secret storage—items that will do double-duty. We've always nicknamed this type of stuff "intelligent furniture"—it will promote optimum flexibility and help you pull the best from your space as required.

Case Study:
Bad Design ...
Guilty as Charged

After

Problem: Is this the place where sofas come to die? Is this really a happy living room where a policeman and his wife enjoy time with their two young sons ... or is it simply another design crime scene?

Solution: A young, punchy design, loads of storage, and a great focal point come together to create a family-friendly room that's bursting with joy!

Before

Plus Points

* Generous floor plan
* An easy-to-decorate rectangular space

Minus Points

* Carpet that's well past its sell-by date
* Poorly positioned furniture
* The room reeks of the past and desperately needs to be led toward a brighter future

After

Great storage makes for great rooms so, with that in mind, we designed this custom installation to provide shelves that are as attractive as the objects they display. When showcased on shelves like these, even budget accessories look stylish and expensive.

The large modern sofa seems to float above the floor thanks to its light-reflecting chrome base and small legs. Leggy furnishings make a room feel larger as they allow light to pass underneath and don't appear as bulky or solid as the sofas that were here before.

The hardwood floor adds an air of indulgent quality and will last and last.

The striped wallpaper (not shown here) on one side of the new focal-point storage area adds interest. Stripes that run from floor to ceiling help increase perceived ceiling height, while horizontal stripes help a tight room seem wider.

We opted for a muddy lime tone to add zest without being too zingy—the colour came by matching one of the strips on the wallpaper. Your local paint supplier will help you match anything you want. Don't be afraid to ask!

Updating the technology helped update the room. The new flat-screen TV easily outclasses the dated TV and corner cabinet.

Plan out your lighting and add a dimmer switch to give you control. Here a couple of well-positioned pot lights illuminate the display shelves beautifully.

Before

C&J'S TIP

Using symmetry and asymmetry to achieve good design is part of every designer's tool kit. Symmetry simply means balance—one side is a mirror image of the other.

Asymmetry is balance of a different kind. The items don't have to be the same shape or size but they should have the same visual mass. So a tall vase could be in balance with two smaller vases that visually consume the same space as the taller vase.

How to Establish Strong Focal Points

THE FOCAL POINT OR FOCUS OF MOST LIVING ROOMS IS GENERALLY ONE OF two things: the TV or the fireplace. We usually opt for the latter as the better choice, but many modern homes now forego a traditional hearth in favour of freeing up extra wall space, so it's the TV that often takes centre stage.

Television as Focal Point

Believe it or not, we're traditionalists and prefer a more typical direction where layout is concerned! We reckon that TVs (not that we want to talk ourselves out of a job!) are best either secreted within a media cabinet designed for this purpose or attractively wall-mounted in a corner. These days several options are available for lessening the impact of the TV. They range from double-door designs to "rise and fall" cabinets that are operated by remote control.

Fireplace as Focal Point

With the fireplace as a focal point, it's particularly rewarding to experiment using design symmetry. Just imagine a gorgeous hearth, the beauty of which is perfectly in tune with your decorative scheme. Then imagine a wonderful mirror floating elegantly above with beautiful identical vases either side. Next, imagine a wall of bookshelves, one to the left and one to the right, providing further visual and symmetrical interest. This, for us, is pretty much the perfect result and a great starting point for the rest of a project. For further drama, we'd consider wallpapering the chimney wall in a design that complements the rest of the room, or we might paint the recesses either side of the chimney enclosure (also known as a chimney breast) in a dramatic shade to really bring the look alive.

We designed a clever solution to allow this modern TV to blend seamlessly with its environment. We reframed one of Laurie's favourite paintings and then added an air-vented lip at the rear which slots over—and masks—the TV screen. *Et voila!*

A regular TV would have undermined George and Margaret's space. Our simple solution was this rather fabulous honey-coloured oak cabinet with a lift-and-drop mechanism contained within. One minute you see it ... the next you don't!

Focal Point Conundrums

What if a TV isn't part of the overall look or if a fireplace doesn't exist? This is not an uncommon situation, and our advice, of course, would vary according to each scheme. Here are some C&J basic principles that will help you along. Let's look at a few specific situations to get you on the road to solving your focal point problem.

Borrowing the Landscape

Perhaps the view to a wonderful garden is your room's best attribute and so, rather than reduce the impact with overly dressed curtains and window treatments, pull the drapes to the line of your window "rebate" (the space where the window frame is set back into the wall) and minimize the drop from pelmets or curtain rods so as much of your wonderful garden can be seen and enjoyed as possible. This simple tip directs the eye to the great outdoors and distracts you from the fact that the room may be a little lacking in architectural features. Simply put ... we always work with what we've got!

Blank Walls

Another way in which we create impact in featureless rooms is to select a wall where the fireplace *should* have been (generally on one of the two walls that lies on a right angle to the window) and then wallpaper this area in a wonderful pattern to immediately draw the eye upon entering the room. A floating shelf (IKEA sells the best ones—look for the Lack series) set at mantle height will trick the eye into accepting this zone as the room's main feature. You can bolster this impression by setting a mirror above the shelf and dressing it as you might a real mantle. You'd be surprised how a little trick like this can make all the difference. We've even been known to paint a matte black block just above the level of the baseboard as a *trompe l'oeil* hearth! Genius!

Windows

With the primary ways of creating focus established, let's look at some less typical

C&J'S TIP

"Pull out" the colours from the pattern in your schematic fabrics and add confident layers of tonal shades to other areas via rugs on wood floors, for example, or scatter pillows on sofas. It's all about creating connective looks that develop a sense of considered design process—posh "design speak" for marrying everything together to make it all fabulous!

methods. Using the *reverse* of the principle that windows that enjoy great views need low-key dressing, it's fair to suggest that if a room lacks features and has a boring view, a dramatically dressed window—perhaps with a couple of layers made up of curtains and a cute blind—can make all the difference.

Artwork as Focal Point

The impact potential of bold artwork is absolutely amazing, but you don't have to shell out a fortune for something by a prominent artist! Could be that the only thing required to bring a room to life is a large blocky canvas in a striking shade. Craft stores everywhere sell simple white frames that can be easily tailored to suit your scheme. In our London apartment, for example, we don't have a fireplace as such (all that remains after some over-zealous renovation by the previous owner is a rectangular niche 12 inches off the ground!), but with a large stretch of canvas that we painted ourselves using inexpensive poster paint, we've created serious drama.

C&J'S TIP

The addition of a simple shelf is a finishing detail that provides for ornament display, and the completed look gives focus to an otherwise simple space.

Case Study: A Living Room Gone to the Dogs

Problem: Is this actually the sofa or is this some sort of giant dog bed? When we moved this couch, we found chewed bones, rotting biscuits, and more pooch hairs than the average Jack Russell has on its whole body.

Solution: Classic furnishings, clean lines, touches of nature, and a pop-art sensibility create a room with serious "wow" factor.

Before

Plus Points

* Interesting raised floor
* Easy-to-decorate rectangular room

Minus Points

* Furnishings are worn, dog-eared, and ready for the dumpster
* Poor lighting
* Artwork hung way too high

After

Try out new colour schemes to create a look that's uniquely you. We used black, yellow, and white—a colour trio more commonly associated with power tools or heavy digging equipment—to provide a pop-art hit in this room.

We created a focal point in a room with no features by decorating one wall to draw the eye toward it. There's no escaping the bold stripes, and the wall dictated where our furnishings would be positioned.

Discover the classics. We love how many "modern" pieces of furniture actually have their roots firmly in the past—these sofas were designed by Le Corbusier in the 1920s!

We always say that adding features adds value, and here the windows have been radically updated with the addition of black custom shutters. Shutters look fantastic and allow great control over how much light enters a room.

We balanced out the severity of the bold stripes, black leather, and chrome by "branching out" and using cut sections of birch trees as a room divider and decorative detail.

A pair of very skinny floor lamps provides handy reading lighting that looks clean and modern.

A modern shaded chandelier adds all the sparkle normally associated with crystal chandeliers but with the added feature of diffused light thanks to the shade.

Before

Storage

IN MANY OF THE DESIGN DISASTERS WE'VE witnessed, the main problem is clutter—an issue that is easily solved. Fortunately, the first step in a design project is to put all that clutter into storage—which usually means the therapeutic process of sorting and tossing!

Analyzing Room-Specific Storage Requirements

Now you're ready to assess your storage needs. Some things to consider:

✳ What bulky items need to be stored—photo albums, toys, electronic equipment?

✳ Future storage needs—do you have a young family whose interests and needs will change over time? As technology changes, can you adapt to more or fewer digital boxes, recording equipment, and so forth?

Think carefully about what it is you need to store *before* rushing out and buying something that won't live up to expectation. If you have to stash dozens of DVDs, for example, make sure the shelf depth of your chosen item will accommodate the boxes before you get your cabinet home. If you're buying a cabinet to stash booze, look for shelves that have a built-in lip to stop bottles from shifting around. And make sure there's enough height to accommodate your favourite bottles. While this advice might sound overly simple, you have no idea just how many furnishing wrongs we've had to right over the last fifteen years! Remember our motto: Think twice, buy once!

Discreet drawer or door-fronted storage is generally the best option as it allows you to keep living room paraphernalia stashed neatly away—and with so many different options available (from free-standing cabinetry to cupboards with hidden compartments and shelves), there's certainly something out there to help you problem-solve.

When we're working with clients, we're proud to explain that our projects are as much about style as they are lifestyle *requirements*. For instance, if working on a scheme that dictates a large quantity of books need to be accommodated, we'll factor in the fact that an average paperback measures approximately 4.5 inches across and design specially built shelves in which literally hundreds of books can be stored. And the best news? Our newly created home library will sacrifice only about 6 inches of floor space—far less than a bulky ill-conceived shop-bought unit. The best solutions are generally the result of careful planning and being brave enough to admit that, even if a piece of furniture is visually attractive, it might not be best for the job at hand.

Storing Bulkier Items

The consumer society in which we live has led to a constant gathering of more and more stuff. Hi-fi equipment, game consoles, multimedia remote controls, or simply a bundle of kids' toys—it's all got to be stashed somewhere when not in use. Smaller items are one thing but, if you need to store larger items, shelving on either side of a chimney enclosure can provide the perfect solution. You can build the bottom sections to the same depth as the chimney breast and add simple doors for this lower section. We like to leave the higher shelves open. Our storage motto is "Double D—Display and Discreet." Even if it means calling in a carpenter to build something from scratch it's worth it. Or, if you'd prefer to limit outlay, compromise and buy off-the-shelf dressers and build around them to fit them into your space. Even custom-built storage and shelving can be surprisingly affordable, especially if you opt for a veneered wood or paintable fibreboard, both of which cost a fraction of solid lumber but are generally equally serviceable.

Future-Proofing Your Storage

Storage needs change over time so future-proof your storage by making it as adaptable as possible. A particularly useful design is the rack system, which even the most inefficient DIYer will find easy to assemble. It's also one of the cheapest solutions on the market. Shelves can be added, storage drawers inserted, or baskets hung as required.

Double-Duty Storage

Maybe it's the Scottish in us but we appreciate good value—we love getting a big bang for our buck! Anything that provides extra service—over and above that for which it was originally planned—is a bonus. If we can get double duty from one piece of furniture, we're delighted, especially if that added bonus is storage. When

you're buying case goods—things like trunks and coffee tables—always seek out designs with hidden compartments or lift-off lids, as these are the ones that will help you use your space most efficiently. Stools with removable tops are great for stashing kids' toys while sofas with concealed drawers are just the answer for storing out-of-season blankets and throws.

If you need to section off areas of your living room (perhaps to mask an office zone or to partially screen the view to a dining area), cube storage—or free-standing open shelving—is a great solution. Indeed the more—or less—you want to mask a particular corner, the more—or less—you need position on the shelves! In short, your ornamentation can be used to further mask each zone.

As is so often the case, the more you're prepared to spend, the more you'll get. Money

spent on sliding doors for living room storage is money well spent. These doors are generally slide mounted in front of standard open shelving so you can reveal or expose your stash as required. They can be rigged up fairly easily using kits you'll find in big-box stores or DIY centres. Paint them the same colour as your walls and they'll almost disappear!

Tech and Multimedia Storage

Unless you've really spoiled yourself with drop-dead gorgeous sound systems by Bose or Bang & Olufsen (who we reckon create the most efficient and beautiful iconic technology), it makes sense to keep your sound and vision equipment discreetly stored behind closed doors. Heard, and *ahem,* not seen, as it were! If you've chosen to have the equipment professionally installed, all the wires and boxes with their

blinking lights should have been discreetly and tidily concealed in a hallway cupboard or living room closet, so all you need worry about is what to watch or listen to! If you have a more everyday system, consider positioning a sideboard below your TV and keeping everything, properly vented of course, within it. After all, who, as they're chilling, really wants to look at an explosion of wiring and cables? If your space is modern, long and lean cabinetry will probably look best; if your living room has a more traditional feel, an antique-style cupboard with double doors might be more appropriate for the job. Visit your local antique market or second-hand store to find good-quality options that can be amended, with a little drilling, to accommodate cables and air passage. Just *don't* put an electric drill anywhere near that gorgeous Chippendale dresser!

Flooring

IF WE HAD A BUCK FOR EVERY TIME SOMEONE asked us which flooring is better—wood or carpet—we'd be very rich boys indeed! The truth is that each of these traditional options, as well as a host of other solutions that we'll discuss below, has a place in today's modern home.

Wood or Carpet?

Believe us when we tell you we don't prefer one over the other. More often than not, we use a combination of wood *and* carpet in our living room projects. While this might sound a little confusing, it's really rather straightforward. We usually lay wood floors and then dress them with large area rugs, which are particularly good at providing definition of function in open-plan rooms.

We're often asked "Which is warmer—wood or carpet?" In our opinion, carpet offers more immediate warmth underfoot as you walk around, whereas wood is the better insulator due to its natural density.

If You Choose Wood

If you do opt for a wooden floor, invest as much as you possibly can to choose a top-quality board that will last for years to come.

Many people choose laminates, but there remains some confusion over what laminate actually is. A proper laminate is a very thin veneer of real timber that is bonded to an underboard of wood composites, and this type of flooring can be fairly serviceable. However, the thinner the veneer, the less likely it is to be able to be sanded or resanded and restained further down the line. But the real problem with cheaper laminates is their construction—often little more than cheap compressed sawdust board topped with an acrylic photograph of wood grain. This substandard floor will neither look nor act like a quality product, and in our experience, it warps easily and soon shows itself as the poor product it is. Yes, it's cheap, but it's not good value, and before you know it you'll be seeing breaks in the surface and movement at the point where the boards interconnect. And if it gets wet? We're talking milk on Weetabix! As our saying goes, "If you buy cheap, you buy twice."

Another far more satisfactory flooring option if you like wood is "engineered" board. This type of wooden flooring is made up of a reasonably thick timber layer that can usually be

C&J'S TIP

If you can afford the outlay, invest in professional floor installation as inexperienced fitting will come back to haunt you as boards separate and levels shift over the years.

refinished, sometimes as often as three times. As always, check product specs before buying as standards can vary dramatically between manufacturers. What's more, because it's made of real wood, it gives the visual depth and warmth you'd expect from the real thing.

If You Choose Carpet

There are so many types of carpet—natural, man-made, and mixed fibre to name a few— that it would take forever to list each one individually. We have found that generally the higher the wool percentage, the warmer it'll be. You have to weigh that against the advantage of a high-quality nylon, though—greater durability.

We *love* pure new wool carpets (hey, they even smell good!), but they're pricey so we often find ourselves looking at less expensive options. But panic not—in this case, just because outlay is less, it doesn't mean you'll have to sacrifice standards. Manufacturing processes these days ensure that even cheaper options are serviceable, and the colour ranges are such that there's sure to be something to complement your scheme. Walking into any one of the literally thousands of carpet mills, flooring shops, or rug warehouses will demonstrate that!

Sea Grass, Coir, Jute, and Sisal

Flooring choices extend beyond wood and carpet. Natural materials such as sea grass, coir, jute, and sisal can add a dramatic twist to your decorating scheme. They provide extra visual and literal texture and come in a range of finishes. These flooring options, often constructed in a chevron or ribbed finish, look particularly good in traditional environments. We have a fondness for this type of flooring—we lived for many years in a house that was floored almost completely in a combo of several of these types! Just a couple of things to bear in mind, however: When these floorings get stained, it can sometimes be difficult to remove the offending marks as it's harder to scrub into the pile. And if sea grass gets wet it can smell a little like—*ahem*—cat wee-wee. So be warned!

Tile Flooring

Whether you're looking at ceramic or stone, marble or granite, the more you pay, the better quality you'll get. When we have an unlimited budget to work with, we love to lavish our schemes with the real thing. When the budget is limited, we're happy to compromise and select from an increasingly massive range of "interpretations"—by this we mean materials manufactured to look like stone or ceramics. These days, it's become increasingly difficult to tell genuine from fake stone or ceramic. Tile flooring is not often used in living rooms, but that doesn't mean you shouldn't consider it. In our Glasgow living room (because we'd invested heavily in other aspects of the design), we had to pull back costs by selecting an interpretation flooring product. The look, however, is so convincing that everyone who sees it comments that "real stone was such a great choice, boys!" As is often the case, it's all in the dressing—such things as coffee tables and accessories—and final styling. Working with the sartorial principle that an inexpensive pair of shoes can be made to look much classier when teamed with a chic little black dress or a smart lounge suit, clever selections are all about "smoke and mirrors"!

C&J'S TIP

If you're tempted to lay your own carpet to save on costs—*stop now!* A budget carpet can look great if it's professionally fitted but an expensive carpet can look really cheap due to inept fitting. Having the relevant stretching tools, knowing how to use them, and understanding the carpet's "structure" are paramount to success. Knowing how much to pull, where to tack, and how to bond sections are critical to good results.

Case Study:
Beach Bummer

Problem: This beach-house room feels claustrophobic thanks to its small size and dominating wood wall, so the overall feel is one of doom and gloom.

Solution: *Hoorah!* Now the perfect place to show that small spaces can also rock—we created a cosy beach theme but brightened everything up with predominantly white decor.

Before

Plus Points

* Older property close to beach so the feel-good factor is high
* Large window floods room with light

Minus Points

* Wood floor in poor condition
* Furnishings poorly arranged
* Wood wall too dominating

After

Adding a chimney breast is a great way of creating a focal point, especially when there are no competing features nearby. It also provides a point around which to arrange furniture so the finished room takes on a new focus.

The river stone tiling brings a beachy feel and shows that subtlety wins over theming any day!

We added painted tongue-and-groove panelling at chair-rail height to cozy up the room and create a gorgeous Cape Cod look. By painting it the same colour as the wall, we let the detail speak for itself.

On the floor we've used Van Gogh Bearwood board from Karndean. It's easy to install and offers the rustic look of sun-dried, salty timber without dirt-hoarding gaps or splinters.

We were inspired by the sea and all things beachy when it came to adding colour. The soft furnishings, cushions, and window treatments are in aqua, sand, white, and natural green tones.

Here's a fab way to keep the coastline clean and get some great free artwork into the bargain. Head down to your local beach for washed-up driftwood branches and allow them to dry in the sun for a salty, baked look. Bracket them onto the wall and you've got sculptural artwork like no other. But don't go overboard, or you'll have to call in C&J again!

Before

Colours

IT'S TIME TO FLEX THOSE FAN CHARTS! THE GOOD NEWS IS THAT getting colour "right" is a lot easier than you might imagine. Getting colour wrong, however, is also relatively simple. We always advise *serious* caution when selecting your palette. Spend as much time as possible considering the character of your living room, bearing in mind that certain variables, such as lighting, can have a dramatic impact on how colour behaves in your space. Dark shades, for example, are substantially brightened by good natural light whereas softer shades can help open up rooms where natural light is limited. It's also worth remembering that the *amount* of your preferred shade will have an impact on intensity. A strong accent wall played against other more neutral walls won't be nearly as in your face as an entire room painted in the same dramatic tone.

Before you even start looking at colours, ask yourself what you hope to achieve, moodwise, in your living room. Do you want it to feel cozy? Or perhaps bright and welcoming? Is your living room simply a casual zone in which you snatch the late TV news before bedding down for the night? Is it important that your space has real design presence and considered aesthetics? *Hmm?* Well … if you hadn't noticed … those last few posers were trick questions! Your space should be flexible enough to tick these boxes so it looks *and* feels fabulous at the same time! Colour can help you achieve the mood that's most important to you, but it's about more than just the paint or wallpaper on walls—good selection should include the furnishings and accessories working together to make a unified whole.

Choosing the Best Colours for Your Living Room

Because the living room is generally the largest space in your house and the area on which you're likely to spend the most money (you'll be buying sofas, chairs, cabinets, and tables as well as all manner of storage solutions), we'd advise a scheme that can be easily changed *around* these biggest-buy items. So, for the moment anyway, it's back to our favourite starting point: neutrals.

We talked earlier about future-proofing storage, a concept that also applies to decor. To future-proof decor, establish backdrops that can be constantly updated as seasons change or as your moods evolve. Many people perceive pure white as a little austere and impractical for families (however, modern paint-manufacturing technology has made cleaning and maintenance of most types much easier), but we regularly specify it as the colour for walls, building colour into our plans in other ways. You'd be amazed at how a large art piece or a colourful sculpture can shine as a dramatic focal point to your living room or how a soft-glow light bulb can add a delicate pastel tone to an otherwise white environment. Or, for that matter, how the addition of simple throws, scatter cushions, and ornaments will immediately enliven the proceedings.

Of course, our *fabulous* guidance is all very well, but do we practise what we preach *chez nous?* Of course we do! In our own homes, most walls are white or one of its many variant tones. But you'd never think of our rooms as

C&J'S TIP

Using accessories rather than paint, a room's mood can be changed on a whim as fashions change.

white—have we added *serious* colour! In our Glasgow living room, people's first reaction is "Oh my God, charcoal is *so* risqué!" The fact of the matter is that only one recessed area is grey—all other walls are pure white. The main graphite impact comes from grey sideboard doors and a host of slate-coloured accessories to which we add or subtract on a whim. Similarly, in our London living room, the bright red scheme is actually a shade of white called bone that covers the expanse of glossy modern wall cabinetry. Why do we say the colour scheme is bright red? To one side of the cabinetry hangs a massive pillar-box red canvas. Lipstick-red cushions enliven a black suede sofa, and Chinese lacquerware in vivid scarlet tones completes the story. And, in our downtown Toronto

penthouse, another white scheme is brought immediately to life courtesy of an ebony floor and loads of shiny black and yellow Italian glassware. Oh, and a bright yellow velvet Queen Anne, pops an unexpected and juxtaposed design element into the room!

So what we've demonstrated is simple: Choose a neutral background for your walls and introduce colour through accessories, artwork, cushions, and other furnishings. These elements are much easier to change than the colour of your walls. Remember those two key concepts: flexibility and future-proofing. As much as we like to think we've single-handedly brought colour back into Canadian homes, we also like to think we've demonstrated how to use colour in a more responsible manner.

C&J'S TIP

Refer to our in-depth colour section (pages 266 to 287) to familiarize yourself with everything you need to know, but remember that good colour selection is generally dependent on room specifics.

Case Study:
Country Bumpkin Style, Big City Living

After

Problem: The room looks like it was decorated by the Waltons but without the country charm! Farmyard style may work well down on the farm but in the big city, it's definitely a case of "Old MacDonald, ee-i, ee-i… NO!"

Solution: Create a sophisticated room with generous amounts of seating, a great modern focal-point fireplace, and a few small details that decorate without dominating.

Before

Plus Points
* Interesting fireplace and window arrangement
* Huge room
* Very clean and well-maintained

Minus Points
* Identity crisis: country in the city
* Dated details on fireplace
* Curtains that look like farmyard aprons!
* Furniture placement leaves centre of room bare

After

The strong focal point fireplace was updated by removing the floral details and by retiling the hearth with chocolate ceramic. If your fire surround has a strong shape, adopt a "less is more" approach. Pare down the details and let the shape speak for itself.

A simple stripe detail is repeated on the curtains, pelmets, and lamp shades to provide coordination. A repeated motif like this makes for a thoroughly considered look.

The three prints positioned above the sofa elongate the perceived length of the room and add a decorative touch to a plain wall. The ideal height for picture hanging is 56 inches measured from the centre of the piece to the floor.

Glass tables are fabulously hip and take up little "eye space." Mixing modern-style tables with traditional armchairs creates a unique style that is modern without being too cutting edge.

The symmetry of two lamps, one either side of the sofa, makes a strong style statement and adds to the balance created by the windows on either side of the fireplace.

The chocolate, blue, and white colour scheme is appealing to all sexes and brings harmony to this family home. A chocolate area rug tones with the colour of the wood floor and adds texture and comfort.

Before

Case Study:
Old Before Their Time

After

Problem: The married couple who live here are a funky and fabulous 50+ pair who were younger than their years in person but much older judging by their decor!

Solution: A fresh new room with classic furnishings and modern touches makes for a scheme that will stay fashionable for years to come—and one that's in keeping with the owners' fun personalities.

Before

Plus Points

* Wood-burning fireplace
* Spacious accommodation
* Well maintained—if in bad taste!—room

Minus Points

* Dated furnishings
* Electronics needed updating
* Drab decor with wallpaper border from another era!
* Brickwork on fireplace breaks up the room, making space feel limited

After

Painting the brickwork to complement the wallpaper was a cash-conscious way of camouflaging it and merging it into the background. It's part of the colour scheme, not in competition with it.

Mirrors bounce light around, making the room feel fresher and more spacious. The sunburst design above the fireplace adds an interesting shape while the three mirror frames hung side by side to create a landscape triptych further elongate proportions. Other metallic finishes like the coffee table legs and lamp bases also bounce light, as does the foil detail on the wallpaper.

Wall-mounted items free up floor space. Not only does the flat-screen TV modernize the setting, it also helps enlarge the room by keeping "foot space" clear.

Use black sparingly for impact and contrast. The black lamp shades, picture frames, and sunburst mirror really illustrate how this works.

The wood-effect plank flooring tones down the coolness of the grey colour scheme and adds a lovely natural touch.

The occasional tables can be moved as required, to be used as a central coffee table or as a pair at different sides of the room. What's more, the clear tabletops serve to visually declutter our design.

Before

Lighting

WE REGULARLY PREACH THAT LIGHTING WILL MAKE OR break a design scheme, and it's in the living room that this designer sermon is particularly relevant. Generally speaking, it's here you'll need to change mood more frequently than in other rooms to accommodate different social situations, so it's worth making the maximum effort to get it right. We consider ourselves past masters with all things illuminating, one of the most rewarding aspects of design. We wince when we see potentially attractive rooms ruined by poor lighting choices. And the worst design faux pas when it comes to lighting? A tired lampshade dangling centre stage from a bumpy ceiling whose rough surface has been exaggerated by the upward glare of a hundred-watt bulb. Gorgeous? *Not!*

To simplify matters, we'll split our subject into three easy categories: task, mood, and feature lighting. Broken down this way, lighting choices become easier to make—there really is no excuse to let your living room be anything other than utterly switched on. What's more, a multilayered plan, which borrows from each of these categories, will cater for practicality and atmosphere in one easy installation.

As with anything electrical (save for tasks such as changing light bulbs!), we'd advise employing the services of a pro for installing lights.

Case Study: Dated Suburban Living Room

After

Problem: This room's owner was a young mum who'd inherited her mum's sofa … and bad taste! Blimey—who'd have thought two crates and a chest could make such an, *ahem*, "stylish" hi-fi unit.

Solution: We specified a great sectional sofa, a zesty colour scheme, and some very defined clean lines to create a room that's young, fresh, and vibrant.

Before

Plus Points
* Spacious accommodation
* Large windows
* Wood floor in good condition

Minus Points
* Mismatched and dated furniture
* Poor placement of furnishings, effectively splitting the room in two
* Dreary colour scheme
* Mismatched and ineffectual drapery
* Poor attempt at DIY hi-fi storage

After

We painted this dingy space fresh matte white to clean it up and create a blank canvas with which to work. If you're decorating bumpy walls or textured ceilings, use a matte finish instead of satin to help disguise imperfections.

Paint isn't the only way to add colour. Here the sofa, soft furnishings, and artwork take things from boring to beautiful. We used orange as our central theme, but don't be afraid to experiment; every colour works well with white.

Inspired by the wooden dividing shelf in the Before shot, we added a storage system at the other side of the entranceway for balance. Details like this really make a difference but cost very little.

To increase the feeling of space and to bounce light around, we used furnishings with a leggy quality—nothing floor-hugging for this project! The white table, sofa, chaise lounge, and swivel chair all sit on thin legs for a clean, modern, and spacious look.

We used the existing curtain pelmet to extend the track to full wall width. The curtains, beautifully bunched on either side, make the window feel much larger, and the fabric adds muted colour while softening the impact of our predominantly white design.

To ensure our colourful home wasn't too "Playschool," we avoided adding extra colours that would have detracted from the impact of the orange elements. Instead, we used natural tones of brown via cushions (and wood finishes like the cube tables) to stop the room becoming too contemporary.

Before

Task Lighting

This type of lighting makes a task or a job easier. It's the most focused light in the room. For example, a directional side table lamp (to help, perhaps, when you're on the sofa reading a book) falls into this category, as does an over-the-desk ceiling-mounted pendant in a study alcove that focuses attention in that space.

Visit any good lighting store (our favourite is Union Lighting—their volume of modern and traditional options is staggering) so you can choose from a mix of styles. For desks, angle-poise designs are super or opt for "mother-and-child" lamps, which shed directional light in two zones at one time. Simple, but *very* effective for practicality and for the visual effects they allow you to create.

Mood Lighting

Your living room is a bit like a stage set—and like a stage, amazing effects can be created with clever lighting. But forget those massive arc lights used in theatres—if we told you that our most reliable method of creating adjustable atmosphere was via a $20 purchase,

C&J'S TIP

In the store, always ask to see lamps switched on and check for the maximum recommended wattage before buying. It's so disappointing to get your choice home, only to plug it in and see that the internal mechanism is visible through the shade or that the lamp simply won't be bright enough to properly serve its purpose.

what would you reckon? That we'd gone crazy? Believe it or not, one of the easiest ways to change mood is by installing a twenty-buck dimmer switch. On all our projects (whether they be TV, magazine, or private commission), it's the very first cost we factor in to our equations. By twisting your dimmer down to a ten percent output, your space will suddenly take on brand-new personality! And don't be scared to mix in a little candlelight to add to the drama. Few things are more atmospheric than a host of flickering tea lights or a few strategically placed scented candles.

Mood lighting can also be used to add a gentle glow to a particularly dark corner, thus softening edges and creating a soothing localized "blur." Try positioning a small lamp behind a large houseplant to cast artistic shadows across a nearby wall, or establish warm ambience by concealing a discreet—small and almost invisible—lamp behind a sofa or chair. If it has a flexible neck, you can change the mood and emphasis by aiming the light at the wall, the ceiling, or straight down. Creating lighting pools like this bring your space alive, particularly in the evening, when mood needs to be carefully tailored.

Feature Lighting

This category of lighting specifically highlights individual features and can be used to draw attention to a particular zone. Generally speaking, it is highly focused and designed to emphasize elements such as artwork or interesting architectural detail. Examples of feature lighting include discreet illumination concealed within glass-fronted cabinetry or along shelves (to highlight contents), recessed directional ceiling pot lights, "washers" (wall-mounted sconces usually shaped as a shallow half circle), or pin spot lamps (lamps with small shades that send bullet-point illumination) that highlight the contours and texture of a beautiful piece of artwork or dramatic sculpture.

C&J'S
Top 5 Tips on How to Be a Lounge Wizard

1 Avoid ostentatious sofa design. Ideally, sofas should be a solid colour—keep patterns to pillows and throws—and practical enough for the entire family. Light covers show more dirt, but the dirt's still there on the dark ones—surely it's better to be able to see and deal with the problem rather than pretend it doesn't exist? Check *before* purchase that covers are machine washable.

2 Avoid textured wall coverings and if your surfaces are already bumpy, hire a good plasterer to smooth out those imperfections. Remember—a little preparation goes a long, *long* way, so spend time preparing your walls for painting or wallpapering by smoothing out imperfections before you start.

3 Pushing furniture into corners will not make your living room feel larger. Instead, create a sense of spaciousness by bringing a coffee table into the centre of the room and arranging furniture around a focal point such as a fireplace.

4 Narrow console tables aren't only for dressing against walls—they also look fabulous positioned behind sofas, especially if propped either side with a gorgeous lamp.

5 Don't be swayed by fashions—just because, for instance, glamour is the big news story in the design world, it doesn't mean you should follow that route. Find a personal style *you* love and stick to it.

Dining Rooms

THE HUMBLE DINING ROOM HAS BEEN IN AND OUT OF FASHION MORE OFTEN THAN BRITNEY Spears. But it's an important room, and one we love to celebrate whenever possible. For decades, even generations, the dining room was the preserve of those with enough money to enjoy the extra space their incomes allowed. In Victorian times they were richly decorated spaces but were for the most part kept closed and used only on special occasions. The dining room was thus viewed (especially by those who didn't have one) as hallowed ground or a secret space that would remain forever out of reach.

Over time, the popularity of the dining room rose and fell as lifestyles changed. When property prices rose, dining rooms became a luxury. Instead of putting money into a room reserved only for eating, cash was spent on more intensively used spaces such as kitchens and bedrooms. The notion of dual purpose took over as a way to provide the dining function. Living rooms with dining areas became common and kitchens tended to be built a little larger to accommodate tables and chairs. People with higher incomes still had houses with dining rooms, but most homeowners learned to enjoy dinner on their laps, particularly as the TV era dawned.

By the middle of the last century, building costs became more competitive and the dining room started to nudge its way back into people's affections. The waxing and waning of the dining room, in fact, is often closely associated with upturns and downturns in the economy— the dining room can be sacrificed to keep housing costs down. Because of this, spaces were often designed to interconnect in a much less regimented way. Gradually, boundaries between living and dining became blurred in the open concept designs that remain popular. In older houses, it became common to remove interior walls to create large multi-use spaces.

These days, as far as we're concerned, the dining room—or at least the dedicated dining space—is officially back! In virtually all our projects, good dining space is one of the first things we consider. As demand for space for entertaining increases, condo developers and home builders are again adding this valuable asset to their floor plans, and we celebrate its return!

What Makes a Good Dining Room?

THIS IS A DIFFICULT QUESTION TO ANSWER AS the dining needs of each project are generally dependent on the people who live in the house. An average family, say a couple with two children, will need more space than a young couple who have fewer people to accommodate daily. However, that young couple might entertain more so their dining requirements might be more formal than the family, who might be perfectly comfortable in a dine-in kitchen. We try to come up with designs that offer flexibility—arranging your dining zone to be changeable at a moment's notice can reap dividends. (See our chapter on double-duty spaces, page 230.)

Ideally, a dining room or zone should offer a relaxing place to eat, space for a proper table, and room for a cabinet or cupboard that can hold the china, silverware, and tableware you use at mealtimes. Note that we said "ideally." If you have a room that can be devoted exclusively to dining, you are in an enviable position and will have room to make the ideal a reality. One important advantage of a separate dining room is that, with the kitchen arranged in another part of the home, you can leave all that dinner party washing-up until later … without feeling you've got to clear up before settling back down! If you are in a less than ideal situation, however, don't despair. Colin and Justin are here to help you satisfy your hunger for the perfect dining room.

Case Study:
Proud, Pink, and Pitiful

After

Problem: The salmon colour scheme and assembly of drab furnishings gave this room an overwhelmingly dull feel. And as for the doll and teapot collection? Time, we explained, to divide and conquer!

Solution: The family who lived here needed a serious exercise in paring back so, for starters, we encouraged them to edit their collection of dolls and teapots. We desperately needed to inject light and style, so we brightened things up with a whole new painted furniture look. Which meant getting rid of all their old furniture and creating a brand-new look from scratch!

Before

Plus Points

* Large room
* High ceilings
* Intact crown moulding

Minus Points

* Dull colour schemes
* Collection hell
* Mismatched and very dated furniture

After

Hard to believe it's the same room, isn't it? Well, it is! Here's how …

Start with getting the basics right. The previous parquet flooring had long since seen better days so we installed quality solid wood flooring as a slick replacement. It's worth investing in good basics that will last through subsequent schemes.

A dramatic magnolia wallpaper (in a subdued colour palette of pink and blue) creates an immediately commanding backdrop for an entirely redressed scheme.

We customized shop-bought furniture by painting it pink and highlighting it with gold to provide visual contrast. Okay, so it's a rather snazzy look, but our homeowners were fun and outgoing and totally got it. Remember … the most successful rooms are those that are appropriate to their occupants.

A simple way of connecting different elements of your scheme is via colour. Here, the new pink-painted dining furniture is further visually connected to the wallpaper via the custom blue upholstery, and our new curtains and blinds provide further colour reinforcement.

We built a solid relationship between detail aspects of our scheme. The crystal in the chandelier reappears in vases, decanters, and even in our choice of tall-stemmed wine glasses.

Before

Kitchen/Diners

THE SCALE OF YOUR DINING SPACE IS important, but if you don't have great square footage, don't think your options are limited. In smaller homes, it makes sense to have an open-plan kitchen and diner—you'll have fewer walls that consume valuable extra inches. To understand this, imagine a compact dining room next to a small closed kitchen. Both rooms are potentially cramped. Now imagine the same two spaces but with the main dividing wall removed. Each previously restricted area now has extra perceived space. You've added only an extra foot of floor space to the combined area but the nature of an open plan design makes it feel like much more. Before you undertake any structural demolition, though, consult with your municipality to check bylaws and confirm the wall is not load-bearing. You might just be surprised at how affordable this type of project can be. Even if you have to install steel beams to

provide support where wall sections have been removed, the "lifestyle" return is well worth it!

If there's room in your kitchen, adding a dining table and chairs is a lovely way to draw hospitality into your cooking zone—great news if you're the social type who doesn't want to miss a trick as guests gather and gossip round the table! From a design perspective, we'd

C&J'S TIP

In a dual-purpose room like a kitchen/diner, try to ensure that added function doesn't get in the way of the primary function. Search out chairs, for example, that slip neatly under your table when they're not in use or look for tables with leaves so size can be reduced or extended as required. Could even be that your table, with proper protection, could double as a secondary food-prep worktop when not needed for dining.

Lighting

recommend mixing up the style of cabinetry and furnishings to subtly distinguish between the kitchen area and the dining area. If you have glossy white cabinetry, for example, consider adding a more natural element such as a wooden table to provide pleasing balance. Flip this notion if you have wood cabinetry to achieve a similar contrast.

GOOD LIGHTING WILL MAKE OR BREAK YOUR DECORATIVE SCHEME BUT in dining rooms it's even more important to get it right as these spaces particularly benefit from good mood lighting. In dining rooms, we prefer a combination of overhead lighting, via elegant chandeliers and shaded pendant lamps, and side lighting, via wall washers and table lamps, positioned to add warm pools of light where required. Lighting at mealtime should be soft, but not so dark you can't see what you're eating! (See our dedicated lighting chapter, page 288, for in-depth lighting information.)

Case Study:
Shabby Shabby

Problem: Small space with a whole load of mismatched furniture. To us, this tiny room looked more like a second-hand furniture store than a warm family dining room. What's more, dual-purposing office and dining functions in such an—*ahem*—discreet way simply made matters worse.

Solution: The single mum who lived here with her cute wee daughter so needed a better space to eat, and with this in mind we set about creating a colour-coded room that featured a combo of great storage and modern dining furniture.

Before

Plus Points

* Good-quality wood floor
* High ceilings
* Intact crown moulding

Minus Points

* Swirled textured ceiling
* Dull colour schemes
* Serious clutter
* Mismatched furniture

After

Let there be light! We chose white as our main colour scheme but zested things up with shots of citrus to bring everything to life.

An extendable dining table can accommodate as many as eight diners (always look for furniture that can do double-duty or grow as required) while the newly open-concept vista between dining and kitchen creates wonderful lateral eye lines.

Positioning a compact cabinet behind the dining area affords perfect storage for glassware and crockery while apertures cut into the drywall provide neat little storage shelves for colourful accessories.

This scheme—because we'd spent the majority of our project budget on the kitchen—was an exercise in financial restraint. Resurfacing the existing floor saved us heaps of cash and allowed us to invest in great quality rugs, which complete the look.

Notice how we've connected the dining space, via orange accessories and colour detailing, to both the kitchen and the living room that connect onto it.

Flooring

FOR JUST ABOUT ANY ROOM, WE LOVE A layered look as far as flooring is concerned. Which is why we generally favour hardwood as a starting point with area rugs to properly delineate space. Where dining rooms are concerned, this works *particularly* well. When sizing your area rug, it should project perhaps a foot beyond the rear of chairs as they would sit when in use. This avoids the front-legs-on, back-legs-off problem that often occurs when the rug is sized incorrectly. And don't think you need to spend a fortune on rugs—stores like IKEA have some of the best options available at extremely reasonable prices.

C&J'S TIP

Trawl through carpet mills and end-of-roll outlets to find good value off-cuts. You can have your choice cut to size and "whipped and bound." This naughty-sounding service is simply an edging technique that turns inexpensive remnants into great value rugs. Again, it's the Scottish in us but if we can find a way to save a few dollars, we will!

Colours

SINCE TIME IMMEMORIAL THERE HAVE BEEN preferred dining room palettes, yet these fall into—and out of—favour on a regular basis. During Victorian times, dining room palettes were dramatic although, interestingly, many people wrongly assume they were painted in muted shades. In fact, Victorians frequently painted their rooms red because they believed the tone would promote digestion and conversation, a belief supported by colour psychologists over the years. Green, too, was popular then as it was considered to promote concentration, which also goes some way to explaining why so many libraries are painted in rich verdant tones.

These days, modern tastes prefer accent walls and feature zones and to pick up (and temper) dramatic colour schemes via tableware and linen. It's amazing how much visual punch can be added with a few bold shots of colour rather than by overwhelming the room with one strong tone. And of course the good old accent wall is easier to repaint when tastes change. To tone down a dramatic scheme, use a paler accent wall, and, conversely, to enliven a more subtle project, choose a bolder shade.

Wallpaper provides huge decorating impact but our secret, as always, is to limit paper application to perhaps one or two impact zones and choose a colour from the background of the paper as a paint colour for two or three walls.

In this elegant room we went to town with a baby blue and soft pink flowered wallpaper design. However, because each of the component colours is delicate and because the furniture is hand-painted in muted tones, nothing jars.

Case Study: Beach Bummer

Problem: Where do we start? That barnboard! *Yuk!* That wallpaper! *Noooo!* And for a dining room … it lacked a dining table and chairs! And just what was going on with that curious display alcove?

Solution: Our challenge was simple—create a fabulous dining room where our lovely young homeowners could entertain friends. Our plan included referencing the owners' love of lumber (remember that barnboard!), but this time via cool new flooring and occasional furniture. And of course we'd have to include a dining set. It was, after all, a dining room …

Before

Plus Points
* Spacious room
* High ceilings
* Structurally sound house, with all lines "true"

Minus Points
* Dreadful dated textured ceiling
* Invisible dining furniture
* Flooring resurfaced nearly to point of extinction

After

Blimey—minor miracles have taken place here! And it wasn't a complicated transformation …

New Karndean flexible wood-effect flooring creates an immediate transformation. Installing a decorative rail at approximately half-height provides a subtle shelf for accessory display while tongue-and-groove panelling seals the beach-inspired feel.

Bright paintwork enlarges already comfy proportions while recessed pot lights and a pale wicker pendant light fixture flood the room with illumination after the sun goes down.

The odd-shaped niche has been simplified, lit from above, and now provides a cute spot to display seaside artefacts such as driftwood and shells.

Note how the colour of our specially painted dining chairs hints at the colour of the kitchen that lies beyond. It's all in the mix!

Carefully selected floral canvases provide an understated finishing detail and an artistic flourish to an otherwise very simple scheme.

Before

Kitchens

FUNCTIONAL, BEAUTIFUL, AND VALUABLE, THE KITCHEN IS THE SPIRITUAL heart of the home, a meeting, sharing space where families can congregate, a community centre where homemakers share in daily gossip … and a beer-dispensing snack zone ready for the next big hockey game!

A good kitchen should cater to the full gamut of culinary prowess, from budding cordon bleu chefs to home bakers and from microwaving single city boys to the average Canadian family—whatever that is! To function effectively, a kitchen should be well appointed and well equipped. And it should offer precisely enough storage for any job thrown at it. In a "roasted to perfection" nutshell: great kitchens have to perform perfectly!

Creating the perfect kitchen takes serious planning but the results (if you get it right!) are well worth the effort and will make you the envy of everyone you know. It's also worth noting that a great kitchen not only repays you every day as it makes your life easier and more enjoyable, but it also pays back in adding value to your bricks and mortar in the longer term.

If this all sounds wonderfully appetizing but possibly a wee bit beyond your grasp—fear not; we can help! Just as a good cookbook can transform a flaccid flop into a fabulous flapjack, so too can we provide all the recipes required to make your kitchen absolutely delicious.

Planning the Perfect Kitchen from Scratch

CHANGING ANYTHING IN THE KITCHEN CAN appear to be a daunting task. But take it from us, if you're going to make changes to the kitchen, don't go for half measures. Roll up your sleeves and be prepared to effectively start from scratch. By working through the following steps, you will see that transforming your kitchen is a methodical and rewarding process. Get out the grid paper and pencil and let the planning begin!

* First measure your available kitchen space and note the position of existing services, windows, and doors.

* Next, work out a plan to position appliances, counter tops, and cupboards exactly where you need them.

* Take note of any changes to services that may be required—such as electricity, water, drains, etc.—but remember that swapping like for like (with regard to positioning) costs less than a complete redesign.

Now that you've got the first design draft done—measuring and sketching in your ideal kitchen—here are some practicalities to consider. What you discover at this stage might lead to some adjustments to your original plan. Even if

you're leaving it to the pros, analyze your personal requirements to ensure you get the very best from your space.

* A kitchen has to be able to cope with certain crucial activities: food prep, serving of same, and washing up. To satisfy each of these functions, there has to be good storage for food stuffs, adequate space to stash utensils, and loads of space in which to work. Think about all these factors before you buy your kitchen furnishings.

* When positioning appliances, try not to group white goods together or your kitchen will look like a washing machine store! Instead, arrange appliances with cabinetry between each, or use integrated appliances for a more streamlined look. This works particularly well in small kitchens.

* For maximum efficiency make sure all functions are close to hand so you don't have to walk from one end of the room to get to the kettle and then all the way to the other end of the room to get your cups and tea bags! Designers always try to create a "work triangle"—a clear and easy relationship between sink, fridge, and stove. This area should be uninterrupted by through traffic.

Case Study:
Old Before Its Time

After

Problem: This small-space kitchen had been cut in half thanks to the run of peninsula base units. And the barn door–style cabinets had more than a touch of the Wild West to them! The overall style was way too old for two funky 40ish artists.

Solution: We repositioned the kitchen units, replaced the rear window with French doors, and installed a snazzy pink-and-steel kitchen that simply oozes pizzazz, not pizzas.

Before

Plus Points

* Kitchen was in a great position close to garden
* Lots of natural light
* Sink, stove, and fridge were well positioned

Minus Pints

* Drab with a capital D
* Too many base units—no circulation space
* Fake wood wall cladding—bad in basements, ridiculous in kitchens …

After

To balance the girly pink cabinets, a custom steel fabricator created seamless steel counters and backsplash. Using just one medium here, and in such an "unbroken" way, really increases the feeling of space.

Great storage makes for great rooms, and in a kitchen it's especially important to have a place for everything. So make sure you include storage for small appliances, pots, pans, and cutlery at the planning stage! Little point, after all, in building something fabulous, only to find that the function of your room undermines your completed design.

Make more of what you've got. The previous rear window provided a lovely view onto the garden, but our home owners had to leave the house by a side door and shimmy along a tight alleyway to reach the garden. Not ideal! Our simple solution was to install French doors (not shown here) leading out onto a cute new deck. Joining inside with out is such a worthwhile thing to do as you effectively double your living and entertaining space during warmer months.

The Scandinavian blond wood floor boards lighten up the room from below to make it feel fresher and more commodious. Importantly, we toned the outdoor deck to match the kitchen flooring to blur the boundaries between inside and out.

Bringing the outside in is easy. Here, vases of fresh flowers dotted around pick up from where the garden leaves off. It's all about the "connection."

Before

Applying the Triangle Concept

Kitchen layouts usually fall into one of four basic layouts—corridor or galley, L-shaped, U-shaped, and island. The triangle can be applied to each of these layouts.

Corridor/Galley

In a long, narrow room with doors at each end, the best arrangement is to create two facing rows of units and appliances with the sink in front of the window. Try to allow at least 48 inches of space between both sides to create a safe walk-through and give ease of access to front-loading appliances. In a really narrow room, the kitchen appliances and work area may need to be positioned on just one side of the room.

L-shaped

The L-shaped kitchen is one of the most popular options as the work triangle is uninterrupted by traffic, and there is generally more than enough room for appliances. The space is defined by a long wall and shorter wall at right angles—hence the letter L. This style is usually found in open-concept kitchen/living spaces.

U-shaped

This configuration works well due to the fact that all working areas remain within easy reach. It's great for small spaces or for positioning at one end of a larger room.

Island Layout

This plan needs a fairly large room to work properly. Bear in mind that the most affordable islands are those created simply for storage or additional work surface. As soon as you incorporate sink space or gas or electrical services, installation costs will rocket.

We got extra crafty by creating an island on castors to enable our owners to relocate it as required!

C&J'S TIP

Although most modern kitchens need modern appliances to look the part, don't feel that traditional-style kitchens have to be traditional—a farmhouse-style kitchen can look quite fabulous with modern, stainless steel appliances!

Kitchen Equipment

THE BEST KITCHENS ARE THOSE THAT ARE well equipped so here's an essential wish list. It moves from the must-haves to the nice-to-haves—you can decide where your cut-off is!

Stove or stovetop and oven

Microwave

Extractor hood for stove

Dishwasher

Fridge and freezer or combination

Kitchen sink

Room air extractor

Special appliances: indoor barbecue, wok burner, steam ovens, etc.

Waste disposal

If you can't fit all these appliances into your space, consider where else you might locate some of them (putting a freezer in the utility room, for example) or go for smart buys with twin functions such as a combination oven/microwave.

Nothing dates a kitchen quite like out-of-fashion appliances so future-proof your design by purchasing classic contemporary shapes. Avoid zany colours and instead favour quality items whose appeal will endure. If all your appliances are the same brand, you'll achieve a cohesion that gives the impression of a thought-through, considered scheme. If you're putting everything together on a limited budget, you can get a quality look by ensuring appliances are in a similar finish—all white, for example, or all steel or even burnished nickel.

C&J'S TIP

Wherever possible, we include below-counter storage for recycling bins and materials, but when space is limited, we recommend dedicated item-specific bins located at the rear of your property.

Case Study: Modern Country Kitchen

Problem: Meanwhile … dated or what!? Apple wallpaper border! *Eek!* Cramped conditions, poor work space, and a giant round table that takes up most of the floor. *Eek, eek,* and thrice *eek!* Oh, and we absolutely love (not!) the potentially treacherous combo of trip-hazard rug and knife block. Scary stuff.

Solution: We created a country-inspired kitchen. However, with our owners' wishes in mind, we ensured that our design was also young and modern.

Before

Plus Points
* Well positioned for dining and living room
* Great window—loads of natural light

Minus Points
* Dated design and layout with diagonal corner cabinet
* Huge stove takes up space
* Large round table is surplus to requirements—the dining room, after all, is open to the kitchen

After

Hand-painted kitchens can be pricey, so to save cash, we used off-the-shelf budget-shaker doors that we hand-brushed. We primed the doors well before painting to provide a sound base. If you want to try this, remember our rule: several light coats instead of one gloopy mess.

We designed a mobile kitchen unit (on wheels!) to provide extra storage and work space. Use any shop-bought kitchen cabinet with a section of particle board attached to the bottom to provide rigidity. Add casters, but be sure to include a foot brake or your new unit will end up more like a skateboard!

Stone surfaces bring a touch of class, but they can be difficult to work with and are very heavy. So we chose a manufactured product (CaesarStone) that's lighter than stone, but more resistant than granite. And the best news? It can be moulded into any shape so it's a great solution for even the trickiest custom-fit project.

When choosing colour, experiment with balance. Get the main elements in first and go from there. Here, as our first step, we selected cabinetry then asked ourselves if we wanted the room to feel lighter or darker. Opting for a lighter shade of green, our design was complete.

Try to create continuity from room to room by using colours, finishes, or soft furnishings that match or complement each other. Here, simply laying the same floor between two adjoining rooms connects zones and makes each space feel much larger. Note—no threshold bars or breaks!

Install integrated appliances wherever possible to keep everything streamlined and increase space. Here, the microwave has been housed below to keep work surfaces clear.

Before

Cabinets: Colour and Style

INSTALLING A BRAND-NEW KITCHEN IS A COSTLY AFFAIR. IF YOU OVERDO things with over-the-top schemes, you are likely to find your kitchen quickly feels dated. Wall colour is relatively easy to change, but changing cabinet and appliance styles is another matter. This is an area where you're making a long-term commitment so it's worth taking the time to get it right.

Colour

If you're confident with colour (and plan your kitchen for the long term), by all means go ahead and use that zesty sunburst orange or vibrant blue. However, if you're renovating for profit or simply aren't too sure about colour, opt for more restrained tones such as white, cream, or natural wood and add drama via artwork and accessories. You'll be able to update your scheme by simply changing accessories rather than starting from scratch every time you want to change mood.

When choosing colour, take into account the available light and select accordingly. The kitchen is a working zone and shouldn't be dark and gloomy. Here are some of our favourite cabinet and wall colours, tones that work particularly well in kitchens. With food being the focus, warm shades such as light yellow, vibrant orange, and mid-tone red will add excitement while enhancing social interaction and improving appetite. Pastel blues and greens can help soothe and heal (they're particularly calm and relaxing tones) while bright yellow is believed to increase metabolism … and even cause tantrums! Could it be the shade of choice for our fellow Scot, Mr. Gordon Ramsay?

Whatever the colour selection, ensure your choice of finish is up to the job—remember that kitchens are high traffic areas featuring heat and steam so use paint that's moisture resistant and easy to wipe clean. Your paint supplier can help when you're choosing paint for the kitchen.

Cabinet Doors

The one place personal taste really shows up in the kitchen is in the door style you choose for cabinets. With this in mind, it's worth investing extra research time. Consider the feel you'd like to create, think about the period of your home, and analyze the style of adjacent rooms. Doing this will make it much easier to make good buying decisions. What's your kitchen style? Traditional? Contemporary? Fusion (a mix of traditional and contemporary)? Here's the ultimate C&J cabinet door guide to help you decide.

Wood Veneers—Contemporary Style

Veneers are micro-thin sheets of real wood that are cut and glued to the manufactured surfaces of cabinetry. Because veneer is so thin, one tree gives huge coverage, and therefore exotic timbers are often available at a fraction of the cost of solid lumber. Exotic varieties include zebrano, burr walnut, macassar, bird's-eye maple, and iroko.

Stainless Steel—Contemporary Style

Who was it who called stainless steel *stainless?* Because—*ahem*—it really *isn't!* It's ideal for professional kitchens or for those who want

their cooking spaces to feel like operating theatres. If you fancy cold industrial chic then this is the one for you. The good news is you can now find spray-painted cabinets with the look of steel … but without the fingerprints!

Solid Wood—Fusion

A natural wood kitchen can have a contemporary or traditional feel depending on door style. Plain flat blond wood doors lend themselves well to modern, Scandinavian schemes, whereas framed doors with detailed carving or scribing will impart a more traditional feel. A solid wood kitchen is a quality purchase and will, if thoughtfully planned, add an enduring, understated, and elegant look to your home. Not to mention extra value at sale time!

Melamine Units—Contemporary

Cost effective and highly adaptable, melamine

doors come in all shapes and sizes and in a huge range of imaginative colours. If dollars are a concern, melamine is an affordable starting point. To give your scheme a more luxurious feel, we'd suggest teaming these doors with an indulgent quality counter top such as granite or solid wood. Remember when you wore those expensive new shoes with that budget suit and all of a sudden it came to life? Same principle! In the future, when money isn't such an issue, you can easily replace the melamine with other doors. Another advantage of melamine is that you can incorporate a couple of colours to highlight different work functions or zones. Simple tricks such as these will lift your kitchen out of the ordinary.

Painted Finish—Fusion

Painted cabinet doors can look fabulous but remember—if your colour choice is over the top, you might encounter problems at sale time. You might love those vibrant violet cabinet doors but you could find yourself in a minority of one when it's time to put the house on the market. However … if your project is all about you and the long term—*go for it!* Painted doors can look amazing but you'll have a better chance of getting the shade you want if you deal with kitchen companies that offer what's called Pantone colour selection, a service that makes colour matching with the rest of your scheme much easier.

C&J'S TIP

Apply baby oil to real stainless steel and polish with a soft cloth to keep it looking spiffy.

Counter Tops

LIKE CUPBOARD DOORS, COUNTER TOP selection will have a huge effect on the look and feel of your kitchen. With so many choices available in varying costs, weight, durability, and aesthetics, it's important to think extra carefully before buying. How will your surface be treated? How will it add to your overall design? And, of course, how much will it cost? To make it easier, here's a pros and cons guide to the most popular surfaces available.

Laminate

The benefit of laminate—a thin veneer of wood, plastic, formica, or imitation stone on a lesser-grade wooden sub-frame—is that it's available in a wide range of colours, patterns, and textures. It's also resistant to stains and knocks and, as far as we're concerned, it's a good value and inexpensive option. The downsides are that you can't cut directly on its surface—you'll need lots of cutting boards—and seams are often visible. Generally speaking, laminates should withstand hot pots being set on them but we'd recommend protecting against accidents by using cork mats.

Ceramic Tile

Ceramic tile can be as expensive or as inexpensive as you need it to be as there are so many choices on the market. Tiles are simple to fit (and subsequently repair), and those with a glazed surface are stain resistant. An important warning, however: Grout between tiles can be susceptible to staining or mildew. And sudden, sharp impacts can crack tiles. On the whole, though, they are durable and easy to maintain.

Butcher Block Timber

Also known as maple block, this product looks wonderful and is very serviceable. It's robust, is easy on knife edges, and will actually grow in character as it ages. Its only real vulnerability comes from exposure to water or extreme heat—if it gets too wet it can swell and split, and hot pans can cause burns, although these can be sanded away. To keep it in tip-top condition, it will need regular treatment with mineral oil or beeswax—a small price to pay for its great appeal.

Solid Surfaces

Solid surfaces is the general term used for fabricated materials composed of acrylic polymer and alumina trihydrate. They can be moulded into any shape by heating the material to high temperatures. Blimey! While all that sounds terribly scientific, it simply means they're flexible and available in a wide range of colours. Seamless finishes and clever tricks like bacteria-busting integral sinks and edging simply add to their appeal. The downside is that their precise professional installation and templating requirement can make them pricey. Also note that surfaces can be damaged by hot pans, and some staining may occur on lighter colours. We have a solid-surface white worktop and sink in our London home, and it's proving a nightmare to keep free of red wine and tea stains!

Granite

Granite is available in a huge range of stunningly beautiful colours and patterns. The toughest of all counter top materials, it's also the least porous and is virtually scratch and stain resistant if sealed properly. However, it can become subject to "thermal shock," meaning that it will subsequently flake if exposed to a hot pan. A bit on the pricey side, and a heavy job best left to professional installers.

Limestone

This impact- and heat-resistant warm stone is available in only a few tones but comes in a variety of patterns, with some more decorated than others. Travertine is similar but has a slightly

C&J'S TIP

Don't be afraid to mix counter styles to create individual results. A timber-topped farmhouse kitchen can look fabulous with marble-topped sections or even a whole marble-topped island! And your polar-white modern kitchen might just benefit from a stainless steel food-prep area to add to the practical beauty of the overall look.

rougher appearance. Softer than granite, limestone is fairly easy to maintain but will require periodic sealing to prevent staining.

Marble

Use this stone to give your painted kitchen a traditional look or wrap it around minimalist units for an ultra-modern twist. Available polished or honed, it needs to be professionally installed and will require special care as it's very porous and prone to staining.

Engineered Stone

Engineered stone offers all the look of granite but with greater uniformity. Resistant to staining, it never needs sealing and can fend off heat and scratch damage. Downsides? It's heavy and has poor impact resistance (meaning it is more likely to break) compared to real granite. Again, this one requires professional installation and repair.

Concrete

This very modern material can be moulded into any shape you require. Once sealed, it's resistant to stains and scratches, although the corners and edges can chip if struck by hard objects. It requires professional installation.

Stainless Steel

Shiny steel will give your kitchen a commercial look and make you feel like a professional chef. Heat resistant, steel is sanitary and easy to clean although whoever named it "stainless" needs a lesson in cleaning! From our experience, it shows up every scratch and fingerprint, although a wipe-down with baby oil should see off most pawprints. This material is best fitted by a professional.

Case Study: Lights, Camera, Clutter ...

Problem: Small room, big clutter. Every surface in this catastrophic kitchen was covered with pills, potions, and paperwork, not to mention all manner of useless small appliances.

Solution: This kitchen belongs to a wonderful seventy-year-old actor who in-line skates in the park and is full of life. Just a shame his performance in the kitchen was so lacklustre. Time for a colourful comeback ...

Before

Plus Points

* Great position close to the garden
* Loads of natural light for us to harness!

Minus Points

* Serious storage issues
* Cabinets in almost derelict condition
* Dated vinyl floor covering
* Dreadful clutter

After

Don't think that colour has to come exclusively from walls. We designed and manufactured kitchen cabinets to create our dominant feature and the room positively rocks. However, if you're the type of person who often changes your mind about design, stick to wallpaper and paint as they're much easier (and cheaper) to change than an entire kitchen!

Composite stone surfaces add modernity, especially if they're installed in a seamless fashion with no huge appliances breaking up the streamlined edges.

The striped wall detail is easy to achieve. Simply apply your base colour, leave to dry, then mask off bands with low-tack decorator's tape and apply the dominant colour.

When we say declutter, we mean it! Lose the mess but harvest all the items that really mean something. The barber's chair (not shown here) once belonged to Alex Trebek, host of *Jeopardy* and a longtime friend of our homeowner. Rather than leave it in the basement to gather dust, we reupholstered it and gave it a starring role in this newly glamorized kitchen.

Integrated appliances provide all the cooking ability of larger drop-in stoves but they take up substantially less room. And the built-in dishwasher (left of the oven) is virtually invisible!

Before

Flooring

THE FLOORING CHOICE FOR THE KITCHEN IS one of the most important you'll make. As you begin this step in the kitchen design, you'll be bringing together two considerations—the type of wear and tear it will get and the design aspect of the choices. The wear and tear your kitchen floor will be subject to is yours alone to assess—are there lots of kids running in and out? Lots of spilled drinks and food? Are you a good but messy cook? Is your floor going to need a daily hosing down or an every-other-day swipe? Will muddy pets be tracking in all manner of outdoor bits and pieces? We're here to assist with design decisions—as well as throw some practical advice into the bargain.

C&J'S TIP

Lay flooring seamlessly between two rooms (avoiding threshold bars) and each space will feel much larger.

Your Style

Before you decide on floor coverings, consider how your kitchen relates to other rooms in your home. Is it, for example, open concept that seamlessly merges into a living or dining room? If so, treat both rooms as one and choose a floor that suits both areas. In this kind of set-up, the style of the open-concept rooms should be similar, so if you're redoing the kitchen but not the dining room, for example, the kitchen style should be similar to the existing dining room. It's worth checking out the sections below on types of floor covering, however, because you might decide to have a different covering on the kitchen floor in an open-concept layout—the kitchen floor will likely take the most wear and the flooring you've chosen for the rest of the larger area might not be appropriate.

If your kitchen is stand-alone, you have more leeway. What's its identity? Traditional? Contemporary? Choose flooring with similar or complementary characteristics to your cupboards to connect your scheme. If your choice of wall colour or cabinetry is light, do you want to add even more light? Or do you want to balance your design with darker elements? Now is the time to think about the bigger picture—don't buy anything as a stand-alone element. Consider everything carefully as part of the bigger picture. Which brings us, once again, to our designer chant: "Think *twice*, buy *once!*"

Let's look at what's on the market.

Vinyl

Vinyl is one of the most readily available kitchen flooring materials. It's hard-wearing, spill resistant, warm, and cushioned and will bounce back from most knocks and spills. What's more, it's one of the most affordable options.

Advantages: Available in both sheet or tile form. It's flexible to use and comes in a variety of colours and finishes. Its shallow height means there should be no door adjustments to worry about. Easy care.

Disadvantages: You'll need to pay for it to be professionally fitted as DIY jobs can look like Freddy Krueger popped by. And that, of course, would be a nightmare! Can be susceptible to heel marks, pet claw scratches, appliance dents, etc.

Wood Laminate

Wood laminate is a popular and inexpensive floor covering, though we think that faking it is best left to bored lovers rather than budget floors.

Advantages: Good-quality versions can be hard-wearing, with some brands guaranteeing twenty years' wear and tear cover. Relatively easy DIY installation. Easy to clean. Available in every wood tone imaginable. But remember—some look better than others.

Disadvantages: Water spills can get into the seams, causing swelling and cracking. These can be difficult to repair and the solution, more often than not in our experience, is to lift the entire floor. Cheaper options can look fake and sound hollow underfoot.

Stone

The most common stones for kitchen application are granite, marble, or slate but they are generally the most expensive options. Stone might not offer the comfort you're looking for as it can feel cold underfoot, but boy—can it look gorgeous! And to counter the chilly feel, there's always underfloor heating!

Advantages: We reckon that stone is utterly luxurious. It looks expensive and it makes for a quality installation. Easy to clean, water resistant, and hard-wearing. We'd generally advise expert installation although with careful effort, good DIY results can be achieved.

Disadvantages: Certain stone surfaces (marble, for example) can be slippery so elderly people or families with young children may want to consider other options. It's also worth remembering that some stone (such as limestone) is more porous than others and can stain easily. In addition, if you drop anything made of glass on it, the glass is bound to shatter.

Tile

Ceramic, porcelain, mosaic, quarry, glass, mirror—these are just some of the many floor tiles on the market. The best news is that because there are so many options available, it's well worth shopping around and comparing prices. Sometimes choosing which tile you want is harder than deciding between tile and wood or tile and linoleum!

Advantages: Huge range to choose from.

Hard-wearing—great for high-traffic areas. Relatively easy DIY installation. Water resistant.

Disadvantages: Can be cold underfoot. Smooth shiny tiles are not suitable for flooring due to their slippery nature. Consider installing a mini-mosaic inset into a smooth tile border. Doing this will add design detail and an anti-slip feature.

Linoleum

Linoleum is often confused with plastic vinyl (discussed earlier) because they both come in sheet form. The difference is that vinyl is made from synthetic material and linoleum from natural materials. Made, variously, from linseed oil, cork, or resin, it has a felt or canvas backing, which makes it environmentally friendly.

Advantages: Huge range of colours and patterns. Warm underfoot. Durable and easy to both install and maintain.

Disadvantages: Some styles are more convincing than others when trying to look like stone or wood so shop around—after all, you don't want a plastic-look wood floor with an obviously printed wood grain.

Polished Concrete

The minimalist's dream—hard, stark, shiny, and bare. It's ideal for modernists and those who are anything but cozy! It's a relatively new flooring option for homes so you might need to look around for an installer. This is not a project for the do-it-yourselfer!

Advantages: Good in any application, even in wet areas like kitchens and bathrooms, although waster splashes can cause surface staining. However, we're all about the organic and reckon a little wear and tear simply adds to overall patina.

Disadvantages: Potentially cold and clinical. Can be problematic depending on how much weight it will add to your floor, although an engineer's report should settle your nerves.

Wood

Oak and maple, both hardwoods, are common choices for kitchen flooring and pine, a softwood, is often used to give a worn effect. Great for both modern and traditional styles.

Advantages: Adds an air of quality to kitchen proceedings. Hard-wearing. Will age well and look good for years to come. If you have basic carpentry skills, a DIY installation is relatively straightforward.

Disadvantages: May need to be refinished from time to time. Food debris can collect in the grooves between each board. Can become stained with spills. However, good-quality product is easier to care for.

C&J'S TIP
Remember that there's no place for carpet in the kitchen! Carpets are essentially thick absorbent fabrics that hold on to smells and spills and therefore become sticky, malodorous quagmires if used in kitchens!

Case Study: C&J's Kitchen Nightmare

After

Problem: If your idea of modern living is a kitchen with half the doors missing, dated cabinetry, and cheap plastic handles, then you *so* need to follow our advice.

Solution: We created a modern, streamlined kitchen with plenty of workspace, bags of storage, and tons of personality.

Before

Plus Points

* Great layout with double galley and dining close to French doors
* Loads of natural light
* Space for dining

Minus Points

* Some of the upper cabinet doors were missing due to a small fire!
* Large appliances dominated the space
* Dated tiled floor pattern

After

We redesigned this kitchen for two blokes whose only input was that it should feel slightly masculine. Just in case they possessed a secret Gordon Ramsay side, we created a scheme with an air of tranquility to calm any potential temper tantrums further down the line! The steel grey doors complement the steel appliances and door handles, and even the spotlights coordinate beautifully.

Because the room was rectangular, we chose rectangular "slab" tiles (rather than square) to provide a "relationship." Laying the tiles from front to back elongated the room and the brickwork effect softened the regimented feel that tiling in rows can create.

The overall feel of this kitchen is long and strong with clean straight lines, so our choice of window treatment had to enhance the mood. To visually elongate the space even further we positioned landscape images on either wall.

Avoid using too many fabrics at kitchen windows as they absorb smells and can be a fire hazard if positioned close to a stove top. We opted for black wood Venetian blinds to provide a crisp solution.

In a funky kitchen like this, it's really important to keep surfaces as clear as possible, so make sure you provide plenty of discreet storage (ditch that mug tree now) or a handy built-in niche for the microwave. If you can, opt for a built-in stove top so you don't interrupt your counter line.

Before

Lighting

WHEN PLOTTING YOUR LIGHTING PLAN, ENSURE THERE'S A good mix of controllable task and mood lighting that's capable of meeting all your needs. One single ceiling pendant is *not* enough!

If installing new cabinetry, work with a professional electrician and plan the location of each lamp using your new kitchen layout as a guide to work-zone locations. Using the same colour and wattage bulbs throughout will ensure that all areas are illuminated with equal intensity.

If you're reworking an existing kitchen, look into purchasing easy-to-fit under-cabinet lights that don't have to be hard-wired. And, if you do have only one single ceiling fitting (see above), fit a ceiling-mounted track spotlight to create more than one directable light source.

Task Lighting

Task lighting, by design, makes a job—or a task—easier. This category includes the following:

✳ Recessed lighting positioned underneath cabinets to illuminate counter work space. Provides even, glare-free illumination to make everything safer. No more sliced fingers!

✳ Lighting inside glass-fronted cabinets—a clever touch that is both decorative and functional. Decorative as it allows you to showcase your best china, and functional as everything in the cabinet will be easy to find.

✳ Stove extraction hood lights that take the darkness out of cooking and reinforce your stove as the warm focus of the room.

✳ Lights in heavy work areas such as over the sink and counter. Here's another place for under-cabinet lights!

Mood Lighting

This category is all about creating atmosphere—don't ignore the kitchen when it comes to atmosphere—and includes the following.

＊ Drop-down decorative pendants that create cozy vignettes. Use them to highlight single impact areas and focal points like kitchen tables or seating.

＊ Directional spotlights—to pinpoint artwork or architectural features around your home.

＊ Dimmable lighting—nothing changes the mood of a room quite like a dimmer switch. From frantic food prep to sexy seduction at the flick of the wrist!

＊ Kick plate lighting—a very modern touch that can reinforce the footprint of your kitchen by creating a floating effect.

＊ Candlelight—not all lighting has to be gas or electric. Candles add a cozy and romantic blur …

Further Illumination …

＊ Be aware of your kitchen style and choose a light fitting to bolster your room's identity—for example, if it's rustic go for wrought iron or if it's modern opt for steel.

＊ LEDs (light emitting diodes) are the latest revolution in kitchen lighting and contain a tiny chip (diode) that directly converts electricity to light. They have a life of between 50,000 and 100,000 hours and produce very little heat, making them much safer than standard bulbs. LEDs can be used to create task, mood, and feature lighting.

＊ No matter how many lights you install in your kitchen, experts recommend circuiting them separately so that lighting is zoned—this allows you to create flexible visual ambience by mixing the various lights at any one time. Make sure switches are fitted at least 12 inches away from sink and taps to stop water coming into contact with electricity. Always ask an expert—electricity is not a DIY area!

C&J'S
Top 12 Big Ideas for a Small Space

Kitchens should be practical *and* beautiful, so in a small space your plan has to be inch-perfect to get the very best from your design. But don't despair—just as small cars don't have to forgo fancy equipment, neither do small-space kitchens have to forgo the finer things that can take them from drab to fab. Here's how to get the best from a small kitchen space:

1 Employ floor-to-ceiling cabinets to pull the eye up and create a towering appearance.

2 Lose the pendant light and replace it with recessed lighting to make your ceiling look higher.

3 Don't celebrate appliances—integrate them! Built-in appliances take up less space than a lumpy stove. And use a built-in or under-cabinet microwave to liberate precious counter space.

4 Ditch the dingy—under-cabinet lighting will open up dark corners and flood your counter top with illumination.

5 Lighten up—use brighter tones (not necessarily white) on kitchen walls and cabinets to help open up the space.

6 Tool up—spec up the interior of kitchen cupboards with plenty of shelving, hanging hooks, built-in bins, drawer dividers, or even a pull-out ironing board! Anything that allows you to use every inch of concealed space will really help!

7 Paint entry doors and woodwork in the same colour as the walls to simplify the area and make it feel larger.

8 Use continuous flooring from the kitchen into adjacent rooms to allow space to "flow" better. And don't use a threshold bar between doors as these will break up the continuous effect.

9 Fit wood flooring at a right angle to the cabinets—this will visually push them further apart.

10 Add clarity—using glass panels on the front of cabinet doors (and lighting them from inside) will add sparkle and make the space feel bigger and brighter.

11 Be systematic with storage—efficient spaces feel larger. Look at your least-used appliances and gadgets—things like slow cookers and deep-fat fryers. If you don't use them, get rid of them!

12 If you really want a table in your kitchen but are short on space, try a folding wall design. Simply fold away when not in use.

Bedrooms

YOUR BEDROOM SHOULD BE A QUIET PLACE WHERE YOU CAN RELAX AND RETREAT, A calming space to enjoy tranquil moments by yourself or with your loved one. Just as importantly, it's the place where you drift off to sleep to rejuvenate, night after night, and recover from the stresses and strains of everyday life. Given that we spend as much as a third of our lives in there (eight hours a night, on average), this space should be tailored to meet precise and individual expectations.

The bedroom—one of our most private, personal spaces—should be designed as the very embodiment of comfort, succour, and sanctuary. And because it's such a personal space it should reflect your tastes, your lifestyle, and your practical, day-to-day living needs. So get ready to indulge!

Knowing where to start can be the biggest problem, as it is with any design project. But don't panic! It's not that hard! Take a look around your bedroom and ask yourself, "Is this a considered, tranquil oasis? Do I feel that I'm ensconced in my own little heaven on earth?" Or do you think that because no one else sees your sleep zone, it doesn't matter that you're in the same bed in which you slept when you were in high school? And your dilapidated bedside tables don't even match? Come on—if you really want to feel indulged and squeeze optimum comfort and beauty from your domestic world, it's about time you upped the ante!

Plotting Out the Perfect Room Footprint

AS WE ALWAYS SAY, "PLAN FIRST—PAINT AND decorate last!" Problem solving is absolutely crucial before you move to the next stage of your design. Before so much as picking up a cushion, measure your bedroom and sketch out a to-scale drawing. Then consider the areas with the most natural light. Next, think about what furniture you need and where you'd like it to be positioned. The success of your new bedroom will depend on the mix of these elements. Worried? *Don't* be—we'll show you the ropes!

Plan your room to celebrate its positive aspects and slowly and surely eradicate (or at least minimize) any negative points. This is the time to cure a "wrong," *before* you go any further. When you get "the bones" right, everything else should slot smoothly into place. For example, could your bedroom window easily become French doors that would lead, come summertime, onto a previously inaccessible patio? Or perhaps the current size and position of wardrobes or closets doesn't allow for freedom of movement around the rest of the space. Or perhaps if your bedroom door opened "onto" a wall rather than "into" the room (by changing the hinge position), your space would feel more generous.

Always remember that form and utility are equally important, but utility precedes form in the planning stage. Now that you've measured your room and assessed its flaws and good points, consider every function you require—bed space, dressing room, reading area, etc.—and map everything out accordingly. Treat the area as one "all-giving" space by using the same colour palette and a complementary design throughout. Don't rush your transformation—your bedroom is an important space. A well-planned slumber zone will give you so much back in return—its careful planning is worth every moment you can find.

C&J'S TIP

We always use newspaper templates to physically plot out each room and work out where everything will sit. It's simply a matter of cutting out shapes from newsprint to represent each item of furniture and trying different arrangements. This is a great way of getting a feel for precisely what the space can accommodate without having to go to the trouble of buying each piece, getting them all home, and then struggling to squeeze everything in.

C&J'S TIP

When looking for furnishings, make sure you record the measurements of each item so you can properly envisage how everything will look back home.

Case Study:
A Really Boring Suburban Bedroom

After

Problem: OMG—was there ever a more boring space than this? Bedrooms are supposed to send you gently to sleep, not bore you to death! Dated, dark wallpaper, terrible furniture, and an overall gloominess made this a bedroom desperately in need of a wake-up call.

Solution: A change of direction, a modern headboard, and some coordinated linen was all it took to bring this bedroom alive.

Before

Plus Points
* Huge window flooding room with light
* Good size
* Space for additional furnishings

Minus Points
* Dated everything!
* There was a smelly, hairy dog pad on the bed
* Strange placement of mirror—on the floor …

After

Although the bed is a standard divan, we decided to "go large" with our headboard and called in the upholsterer. To save your loonies, grab a sheet of fibreboard, buy some foam, root out your staple gun, and select your fabric.

Using mirror finishes is a great way of lightening things up without taking up too much "eye space." The previous dark furnishings absorbed light and made things gloomy, but now light reflects from each piece, making everything feel incredibly bright and fresh.

We specified natural seagrass to add to the coastal vibe. If you're putting together this kind of look, use a major element—like the colour of the floor—to help dictate other colours. Our choice of floor helped us pick a similarly blond wood frame for the footstool.

Keep it light, casual, and summery by mixing styles and avoiding uniformity. Straight-line furnishings with ornate detail, lots of clear glass, and small friendly arrangements of fresh flowers provide good detail.

If you crave patterns but want a coordinated look, mix it up a little by using a design that's available in various compatible colours. Here, the headboard has a red background with white flowers but the bed cushions and footstool have a white background with red flowers.

Before

Planning the Perfect Bedroom

WE'RE GOING TO WALK YOU THROUGH THE process of planning your perfect bedroom. It's not that hard … just put one foot in front of the other to take the first step!

✳ Decide what your focal point will be. Is it the bed, a huge armoire, or a dramatically dressed window? Focal points are large fixed features around which you can dress other furnishings. In most cases the bedroom focal point is the bed, so make it a good one!

✳ Next, decide where you want the bed to go. We tend to put the bed on the largest unbroken wall diagonally opposite the door. But different room shapes call for different approaches so practise until you find the best spot. If space allows, throw caution to the wind and try

angling the bed in a corner to completely change the perception of your room!

✳ Now think about where to put your clothes storage. Elements as large and solid as free-standing closets work especially well sited behind the bedroom door, out of immediate eye line. We always look at the wall shape and, if required, use closets to square off irregular or awkward corners. Try to avoid cluttering window walls with closets as positioning them too near the window will restrict the amount of natural light coming in.

✳ At the planning stage, make sure you have electrical sockets on each side of the bed and factor in a way to turn off overhead lighting from the bed. Remote control switches work

well (and are surprisingly inexpensive). While you're at it, fit a dimmer switch to enable you to change mood on a whim.

✳ If you have the space, think about positioning a storage chest at the foot of the bed to provide a valuable stash spot for blankets or sweaters. Pop on a few cushions and you'll create somewhere to sit when you're getting dressed. Or set a pair of vases on the floor next to it and suddenly you've created a vignette with a valuable surface upon which to dress accessories.

✳ Equip each side of the bed with a nightstand and lamp. This won't simply add symmetry, it will also provide a handy place for an alarm clock, a good book, or a glass of water.

✳ Add a comfy chair or chaise longue to provide somewhere to sit when dressing or to create a quiet corner in which to escape the family! Think about the features you might find in a hotel room and adapt them to your bedroom for a feeling of real luxury.

✳ Try to keep your television and audio equipment hidden in an armoire or in fitted wardrobes for that "hotel at home" feel. The trick is to have a well-equipped and furnished room that isn't cluttered with furniture or equipment.

✳ Scour stores and antique markets for unique accent pieces such as unusual dressers or bedside tables—these will add interest and stop your bedroom from looking like everyone else's.

Case Study:
Let the Sunshine In!

Problem: Just pop the deceased over there, please! *Aye*, a corpse is all this bedroom needs to complete its deathly look. Mind you, even the dead would rise again to escape this zombie environment. We added our own "Lazarus" effect with a punchy new colour scheme …

Solution: Ditch the drab and make it fab with a new colour scheme, a great new bed, and spot of reinvention of the existing furniture.

Before

Plus Points

* Well laid out with plenty of space
* Lots of storage
* Lots of natural light

Minus Points

* Wall colour absorbs light to create drab feeling
* Poorly dressed bed—no colour coordination, no headboard
* Dark furnishings add to the gloom

After

The centrepiece of any bedroom is the bed, and here we opted for a modern interpretation of a traditional four-poster. We like its clean, straight lines and love how it adds to the overall design without being overbearing or old-fashioned. We found it in a flat-pack big box store and sprayed it pure white to personalize it.

Some of our favourite pieces of furniture have come from charity stores and have had new life breathed into them with a little creative know-how. Here, we reused the furniture by sanding it down, cleaning it off with a sugar soap solution, and spraying it white to match the bed. We reused the existing handles but added a bit of luxury by topping each piece with black granite.

Sometimes you just have to push the boat out (for non-Brits, that means spending more than you usually do), and that's what we did by using a classy wallpaper shop for this wall covering. The pretty leaf pattern is warm and uplifting, the perfect antidote to what was there before.

Panelling automatically makes a room feel posh, so this boring suburban bedroom now looks like a wonderful master boudoir in a plush hotel. This kind of detail works better in larger rooms although it can work in smaller spaces if you keep it simple.

The 1980s sliding wardrobe doors (not shown here) were horribly dated so we replaced them with panelled doors, painted white to echo the walls. Buy inexpensive plain wood doors and provide traditional appeal by panelling with the same product used on walls.

Before

Buying the
Right Bed

THE MOST IMPORTANT THING IN A BEDROOM IS THE BED. MOST PEOPLE LIKE TO HAVE as big a bed as possible, but you want one that leaves enough "walk space" around either side. If you and your partner are accustomed to sleeping on a 53-inch-wide full-size double mattress, each of you has only 26.5 inches of personal space, about the same width as a baby's crib. Surprising, huh? And you may find that standard length (75 inches) is simply too short. Add to this the fact that recent sleep studies suggest we turn, on average, between forty and sixty times a night!

Queen-size beds are approximately 60 inches wide by 80 inches long, which makes them approximately 6 inches wider and 5 inches longer than a full-size double mattress or bed. You'll find that these additional inches make all the difference in comfort, which probably explains why the queen size is the most popular mattress of all. It's perfect for regular master bedrooms, guest accommodation, and single sleepers who simply want a bit more space.

King-size beds typically measure 76 inches wide by approximately 80 inches long, and these extra dimensions provide an average couple with as much personal space as each would have on twin beds. More space clearly equals more sleep time, not to mention roomier conditions for long lie-ins and luxurious proportions for breakfast in bed!

C&J'S TIP

Take a tape measure with you on your shopping trips to avoid costly mistakes! Always calculate whether there's enough room to get your big buy through doors and hallways and up stairwells.

Case Study: Naughty and Not So Nice ...

After

Problem: Talk about a 1970s nympho porn palace! Big room, big problem—this dated bedroom suite had long since seen better days and was well overdue for an update.

Solution: We created a bedroom that's perfect for a sophisticated young woman in her forties.

Before

Plus Points

* Huge space
* In sound condition
* Lots of lovely daylight

Minus Point

* Incredibly dated

After

To create the wall banding, we used our tried-and-true trick of applying masking tape and painted jaunty stripes rather than shell out for pricy wallpaper. Here's how—first we painted everything with budget white latex and left it to dry overnight. Next we taped out "banners" and then added the blue shade.

More painting—we bought the bedroom suite second-hand, then painted it with pure white eggshell.

It's well worth plotting out where your furniture will go before rushing out and buying lighting. Here, we used white directional spotlights to pick out the window drapes and

then added hanging chandeliers on either side of the bed for a bit of good old crystal-encrusted drama!

We hung mirrors on each side of the bed to bounce light around and to reflect our chandeliers. This lovely balance reinforces the symmetry of the bedside tables and creates a strong visual effect.

Grand French-style comfort is the key ingredient of this look, so—if you've got space—try to accommodate a couple of bedroom chairs to provide a tranquil haven from the rest of the family.

Before

Colour

AS WITH ANY HOME DECISION, IT'S important to properly research your colour scheme. Are there colours that you naturally find reassuring? Is there a shade of soft pink that takes you back to childhood and reminds you of your comfort blanket? Or is there a tone of yellow that immediately makes you reminisce about your favourite-ever overseas holiday? Aye, if you *care*, make sure it's *there!*

Choosing a Colour

Gentle blue is a popular choice for bedrooms as it promotes calm and serenity. Some studies have shown that this shade will help calm a fast-beating heart. Perhaps blue could improve your health and lull you to sleep!

Green is another popular bedroom choice as it's perceived as the colour of the great outdoors. What's more, it imparts a relaxing and rejuvenating atmosphere—colour psychologists explain it's the perfect choice to help calm a child who is prone to tantrums. (Blimey—would it work for us?) Use lighter shades to create a clean look by day and relaxed ambiance by night, and select darker greens as pattern or accent colours.

If it's excitement you're after, then opt for an energetic vibe with red and orange. The vibrancy of these colours awakens the senses in a dramatic and memorable way. Red is also the colour of conversation (in days gone by, Victorians painted their dining rooms this shade to promote good after-dinner discussion), but it's

also good for, *ahem*, seduction! So, if you like to chat or get up to all manner of who-knows-what in the boudoir, this is the colour for you!

Sandy or golden shades are also perfect for the bedroom. The colour of sunshine, they promote joy and a feeling of well-being. By day, a room painted soft yellow will feel lively and cheerful while during the evening the same room will feel homey, relaxing, and snug.

Black is perfect for moody teenagers intent on rebellion … and long lie-ins. Use too much, however, and your room may feel small and oppressive. White, of course, has the reverse effect, effectively enlarging and lightening space. However, if you use too much, snow blindness will occur and the results will be far from restful. Mix black and white and the crisp monochrome contrast can be invigorating, clean, and strong.

Using Colour

Think about a cup of black coffee—add a drop of milk and the colour gets lighter; add some more, creamier still. Your room is your coffee cup—the more of one colour you add, the more dominant it becomes. If you add too little colour, the effect of that one colour will be too strong. The trick with colour is balance. Start with a base room shade, then add darker tones to moody it all up or lighter tones to freshen the environment.

If you're tempted to try a bold, brash shade, but not confident about how much to use or where to use it, introduce it in a temporary manner via window treatments or bedding. Dramatic red linens, for example, will look big and bold (even in a neutrally decorated room) and can be easily changed to increase or tone down the drama as required.

The golden rule with bedrooms is to make them relaxing so avoid garish colours and opt for a tonal, muted approach. Spoil yourself and go wild with quality scented candles, comfy cushions, and soft lighting. It's all about the indulgence—you'll love yourself in the morning!

C&J'S TIP

Leave lots of breathing space between dramatic elements and your room should balance perfectly. If your room is fairly small, rein in any impulse to cram in too much furniture.

C&J'S TIP

When dressing a bed, make it a tactile feast for the fingers as well as the eye. Mix soft satin with cool cotton and top the lot with a luxurious cashmere throw. Then, and only then, will you discover the true meaning of being "good in bed"!

Case Study:
Perfect but Ugly!

After

Problem: Even though these homeowners had managed to keep their bedroom fittings in perfect condition thanks to years of careful use, love, and affection, the pieces still aged and now they look about as modern as your grandmother at a rave.

Solution: Create a bedroom with a quality-hotel, hideaway feel that's ornate and traditional without being stuffy. It's a room they can preserve for the next thirty years!

Before

Positive Points

* Massive master bedroom
* Separate dressing room
* Flat walls
* Great condition

Minus Points

* Horribly dated
* The stallions-on-the-wall idea of masculinity went out with *Saturday Night Fever*
* Too much spare space

After

The look we wanted was one of quality and comfort. This was achieved by using traditional furnishings and fabrics with a heritage feel. Your bedroom is your most personal space and should be where you spend both time and money!

The bigger the bed, the better! Not only was the double that was here before dwarfed by the room, it was also a cozy squeeze for its

occupants. So we upscaled and added this stately king-size bed to increase the comfort factor and add a real style statement.

In a large bedroom like this the trick to furnishing is to plot out certain tasks for certain areas; here the bed is housed against the farthest unbroken wall with bedside companion tables and an ottoman—this is the sleeping zone. At the window (not shown here), a mirrored table and ornate padded seat create a beautiful vignette, while two chairs and a dresser complement the dressing room next door.

Area rugs help to break up the expanse of flooring in large rooms and serve to reinforce the function of each zone. They also add softness and warmth to rooms with a hard floor finish.

Before

Making Your Bedroom Feel Larger

SIZE *IS* IMPORTANT IN THE BEDROOM—IN terms of space, of course!—so why is it that some "normal"-sized bedrooms appear so tight and boxy whereas other (and in fact smaller) bedrooms appear to be bigger, brighter, and much more appealing? Could it be the wrong choice of furnishings? The lack of order? Or simply too many things going on in too small a space? Whatever the reason, there shouldn't be any excuse for having rooms that feel less than spacious and light. Here's a simple C&J guide that will show you how to take a normal-sized bedroom and make it feel positively palatial!

Go Leggy: Less "solid" items take up less eye space so avoid bulky pieces and opt for a bed with legs and a spindly headboard to help you furnish without suffocating space.

Off the Wall: Wall-mount compact shelves to provide a "nightstand" at either side of the bed. Presto—you'll avoid cluttering up the floor. And while you're at it, add a couple of wall-mounted lamps to keep those surfaces clear!

Lighten Up: Could be that your choice of colour is the only element that's letting down your overall scheme. If this *is* the case, lighten up with one of the new army of neutral tones such as the softest lemon or gentlest green.

Change the Bedding: Think about just how much of your boudoir's identity comes from the duvet cover. Freshen it up and the whole room will follow suit and look brighter and larger.

Reflect on the Situation: Mirrors are a great way of bouncing light around. And they don't have to be used exclusively over your dressing table or on your wardrobe doors. Think about hanging a dramatically framed mirror to create a brand-new focal point, or adding floor-to-ceiling mirrored panels to enhance otherwise overlooked architectural features such as either side of a chimney breast.

Keep It Simple: Your window area will feel much larger if you simplify its dressing. So lose the huge drapes and replace them with a smart single blind. It's like the difference between a woman in a little black dress or the same woman in a crinoline frock. That's right—swags add bulk!

Put It Away: Adding a seamless bank of wardrobes down one wall will keep all your clothes and personal possessions hidden away. Yes, you might lose a little in floor area, but you'll gain the illusion of space. You can also incorporate your bedroom TV into an integrated media storage as part of your wardrobe set-up.

Lose the Clutter: Less stuff equals more space. Fact!

Quality over Quantity: If you have a small "spare" bedroom close to another compact room, combine both spaces and spoil yourself with the resulting *huge* bedroom! Or perhaps that unused guest room could be brought to life as an ensuite bathroom or an indulgent dressing room? It's all about exploring opportunities …

Unify: Using the same floor coverings from hallway to bedroom will make both areas feel much larger especially if you do it seamlessly, without a threshold bar (the piece of wood sometimes found on the floor at the bottom of a door between rooms).

Case Study:
Beach Bummer

Before

Problem: Were our homeowners running a private sauna from their master bedroom? And just what was going on with all that knotty pine? But there's more! The textured ceiling was a disaster, the ceiling fan was terrifying, and as for stuffing that bed in a corner when there was plenty of room centre stage? Come on!

Solution: Our challenge was to create a wonderful master bedroom in this cavernous space. We planned to brighten the room by painting the wood and hanging sunny blinds at the windows. Seagrass flooring and a dramatic new four-poster bed would provide exciting design direction. Yellow would give dramatic contrast while stripes would create a properly interior-designed feel. And a new fan would swirl things around!

Before

Plus Points

* Cavernous proportions
* Good ceiling heights
* The awful wood could be easily disguised

Minus Points

* Too much knotty pine
* Textured ceiling
* Poorly chosen and poorly positioned furniture

After

Our initial thoughts of pulling down all that wood were soon replaced by another plan. To make the project as affordable as possible, we sanded, primed, and painted everything white to create a cool-as-you-like beach house feel. And the results, we hope, speak for themselves.

We picked up a factory clearance bed for an astonishing $550 and painted it white. After carefully applying masking tape to create a banded design on the head and foot boards, yellow was applied to create a gorgeously individual look. Maximum results for minimum input!

Replacing hard floor tiles with tactile seagrass provides beautiful results that are surprisingly hard-wearing. We reckon that this flooring is good for at least fifteen years.

Because this bedroom space is so large, we were able to create a secondary living area beside the windows. A squashy sofa and simple artwork create focus and provide a simple nook in which to relax.

Before

Storage

IT MAY SOUND BORING, BUT THE KEY TO A successful room is successful storage. Indeed, the only thing that stands between a bedroom looking like a charity shop after a hurricane and a restful tranquil space is having a place for everything so that everything can be in its place. Great storage makes for great rooms—period. This is especially true in a bedroom, where most of us store everything we wear.

With an element as large in stature—and investment—as a closet, it's worth writing down exactly what you expect to achieve and making sure your solution is up to the task. That way you won't be disappointed after you've dished out your dollars. Specialist closet companies can do all the work for you (Simply Closets is our favourite and we use them on many of our shows) or you may wish to DIY with flat-pack furniture from somewhere like IKEA. Whichever option you choose, make sure, as always, that you "think twice, and buy once!"

Put an end to your wardrobe worries with the following neat ideas:

※ **Keep everyday items within easy reach.** Position regularly used kit at the centre and front of your closet to avoid having to rake through less frequently used garments. Doing this will save time and make your space more efficient. Use higher and lower shelves for seasonal or occasional wear.

※ **Group clothing by function.** Store your sports gear in one area and your work clothes in another—this effectively "merchandises" your wardrobe and makes getting dressed easy and stress free.

※ **Don't waste an inch of available space.** To maximize, add storage units wherever possible and divide the area into a variety of stash zones to handle all clothing requirements. Hang rails at varying heights (for half- and full-length garments). Incorporate open shelves and install loads of drawers and pigeonholes to help use your space more efficiently. Place shoe racks at the bottom level and put pegs on the wall to accommodate scarves, ties, and belts.

※ **Make it visible.** If you can't see an item, you're likely to forget it's even there! So, with this in mind, try open shelves, wire bins, or glass-fronted drawers.

※ **Use doors with maximum access and minimum footprint.** Hinged doors will provide optimum access to your wardrobe, but they may not be ideal for tight spaces as they swing into the room. Sliding doors work in tighter confines, but you'll only be able to see half of your wardrobe at any one time, while good old

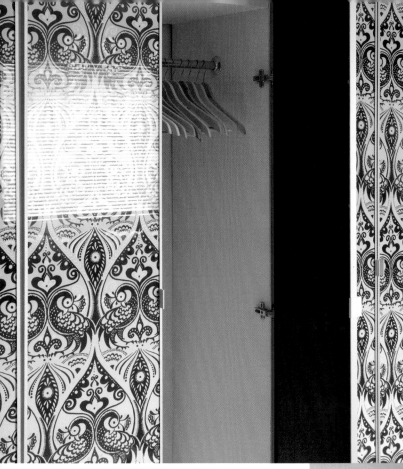

Leave room to dress. Try to have a chair and mirror close to your closets and, if you're lucky enough to have a dressing room, add an ottoman so you can sit down to put on shoes.

Light up your life. For maximum illumination, add a full spread of pot lights to a dressing room and position low-wattage lamps or battery-operated bulbs in your free-standing wardrobe so you can wade easily through contents!

Don't assume flat pack is cheaper. When you add up the cost of dividers, shelves, modular units, and accessories, you might find that a professional installer could have done the job for the same price! Custom cabinetry is becoming much more popular (and therefore far more competitively priced) as it allows you to fit your closets into whatever size and shape of space is available.

bi-fold doors are a nice compromise. Before buying any storage units or hardware, study your potential new closet and analyze where it will ultimately be positioned in relation to doors, windows, and clearance. Will opening and closing its doors conflict with the door to the bedroom? Will it shut out light if it's too near a window?

Let it breathe. Don't overpack your closet as this creases garments and traps moisture. Installing a fan, especially in a closed-door walk-in closet, will increase airflow and reduce the risk of mould or mildew, which even in fairly dry Canada can still be a problem.

Slim down. Be ruthless and lose the things you no longer wear. And learn to seasonally adjust your clothes as the climate changes. In winter, for example, vacuum-pack summer garb until the mercury starts to ascend.

C&J'S
Top 10 Tips to Turn Your Nightmare Bedroom into a Heavenly Haven

1 Always have a mirror handy. Hang one over the dresser or position a full-length cheval or mirror, centre stage, to create an elegant focal point.

2 Don't let the bedbugs bite—air your bed and turn and vacuum your mattress every couple of weeks to ensure dust-free slumbers.

3 Don't air your dirty laundry—invest in a large stylish basket to keep smelly smalls away from prying eyes.

4 Satisfy your sense of smell with relaxing scented candles or some good old-fashioned fresh air. Even in the winter months, get into the habit of airing your bedroom for at least a few minutes each day.

5 When designing your bedroom, make sure it's cozy and restful. Avoid bright colours—like vivid orange and zesty yellow—as these shades won't induce sleep. Neutral, pastel, and warm tones are much more restful.

6 Loads of cushions piled high on a bed can look great but don't do this in a small bedroom—they add too much detail and are difficult to store when not on display.

7 Position your bed diagonally opposite the entrance door on the largest unbroken wall and make that your "feature" wall.

8 Opt for warm flooring such as wood and carpet and avoid ceramic tiles, marble, or granite. There's nothing worse, after all, than getting out of bed in the morning and stepping onto a chilly floor.

9 Don't forget the importance of lighting as you design—it's instrumental to creating an indulgent and flexible mood. Functional lighting should be used to create overall mood while decorative lighting will add interest and act as a design element in its own right.

10 Ensure night stands are scaled properly and positioned within easy ergonomic reach of your bed. Having somewhere for lamps, a clock, and a glass of water is really important

Family and Rec Rooms

YOU'RE A LUCKY LOT, YOU CANADIANS! YOU GET TO LIVE IN A BEAUTIFUL country with some of the most stunning landscape in the whole world *and* you get to claim the BlackBerry—not to mention Céline Dion—as your invention. What's more, you get to live in homes that are generally larger than your British counterparts, homes that often feature many more rooms and an extra floor in your—frequently maligned—basements.

Far too often, this potentially positive asset is a room that looks battered, bruised, neglected, and unloved. Overstuffed with a mismatched collection of inherited sofas and family junk, it's a fall-out zone with all the messy allure of a second-hand furniture store. Less frequently, we see the comfortable well-planned spaces that satisfy the needs of *all* family members while still managing to look stylish and of the moment.

Getting from Wreck Room to Rec Room!

OUR FIRST WORD OF ADVICE IS—*PURGE!* Many family room spaces are crammed with a ramshackle selection of furniture (most of which never gets used) so either give it away or send it to the dumpster. Your space is simply too valuable to allow it to become crammed.

Once cleared out, be ruthless about everything else down there. If you haven't used it or looked at it in a year, what's it doing there? Toss it! Or donate it! It's not hard once you start and it makes you feel better.

The open space you've created will inspire you with ideas about how it can be divided. Assess what you want from the space—is it a room for watching TV, pursuing hobbies, using as a study or office? How about adding a luxurious spa bathroom? How much space can you devote to storage for out-of-season clothes and other items? Be realistic—don't try to cram too many rooms or areas into the space available or you'll end up making another monster.

Dealing with Low Ceilings

One of the most challenging things to deal with in a basement is the fact that ceilings can be on the low side. Fortunately, there are ways to overcome this problem, but money and time will be important considerations.

The most difficult (yet definitely the most successful) way to counter this is by digging down into the soil beneath the existing floor to improve ceiling height. If you're going this far, talk to your contractor—and you must have a contractor, as this is not an undertaking for any but the most experienced DIYer—about installing damp-prevention membranes before the new floor is installed. You'll never regret it. However there are some important warnings:

* Remedial tactics such as these will require a permit.

* Basement excavation can, potentially, undermine the structural integrity of your home—which is, of course, *very* bad news. You'll likely need to underpin your home and then damp-proof the entire basement area to protect against water ingress, as mentioned above.

* It is likely to be an expensive undertaking.

* You'll have to rewire, replumb, and redecorate the entire area.

On a more cheerful note, digging deep can be fantastically effective because of the increased height and roominess you'll gain, not to mention the advantage of damp-proofing.

Lighting

LET THERE BE LIGHT! OR NOT, AS THE CASE SO often is in Canadian family rooms. Problems with natural light go hand in hand with low-level living, especially in "true" basements, which are built mainly below ground level. Homes built on gradient plots are easier to work with as their rear rooms often have full-length windows and in many cases French doors that open onto the garden.

But the big challenge is usually to substantially brighten proceedings and often without interfering with head height.

Here are some ideas to get you started:

✳ If the construction of your basement allows, install recessed pot lights instead of pendants. These lights can be used for general lighting, as well as focusing on a particular feature.

✳ If room height allows, shallow ceiling-mounted track lighting can be used.

✳ Wall-mounted side lighting or "wall washers" give a gentle spread of even light over a wall.

Colour

DRAMATIC COLOURS GENERALLY MAKE SMALL spaces feel even smaller. So it goes without saying that the shade selection for basements is critically important if you want to open things up. We're not suggesting you paint everything polar white in the basement, but it's best to limit bolder colour to easily changeable accessories and ornamentation. What's more, applying big bold shades won't only darken your space, it will also limit your design flexibility.

If you've fallen in love with aubergine, for example, we know from experience that you'll regret splashing it on the walls. Instead choose a decorative palette of softest cream with aubergine *accents*. Shift a few pillows, add a differently coloured sofa throw, change artwork, and all of a sudden your winter-warming purple scheme has become … cream with spring-green accents. Job done!

Flooring

DAMPNESS AND BASEMENTS SEEM TO GO TOGETHER, AND it's a combo we pay heed to when we're thinking about flooring options for basements. Mould is the great concern— it can affect your health as well as the materials used throughout the construction. For this reason, we tend to avoid wood floors unless we can be absolutely certain there's no possibility of moisture transference or damp from the ground below. The boards in a wood floor will expand because of damp, and once this has happened, the floor is never really the same again as the structural integrity of wood is undermined by previous buckling or twisting. (This is why we also avoid using wood floors in bathrooms.) Wood types such as teak or bamboo are much more resilient in the face of water damage but on the whole we'd recommend against their installation.

Carpet is a potentially serviceable option—it's warm underfoot in colder areas such as basements but, once again, it has to be properly protected against damp. We don't want to be harbingers of doom but pretty much any flooring choice (whether wood, carpet, or tile) needs to be properly insulated against moisture penetration or problems will occur. If you choose carpet, your best choice is one with man-made content (fifty percent acrylic and fifty percent natural fibres is a good figure to aim for) as it will be more resilient against moisture and mould than an all-wool product will be.

Our preferred flooring option for lower levels is tile. Whether slate, ceramic, or stone, tile provides a hard-wearing finish that is less likely to succumb to damp problems than other flooring products. To warm things up, we'd advise using rugs with anti-slip pads placed underneath. Before tile is laid, don't forget to install damp-proofing. After the tile is laid, a protective clear coating with a mould inhibitor can be applied. Speak to your installer for information or have a chat with the crew at your local DIY store for advice on the best product for your job. The solutions to the problem of damp have improved greatly over the years and continue to be refined.

Case Study:
Tartan Terror

After

Problem: Okay, so you know we're two proud Scottish boys, but even we were unhappy about this terrible tartan decor! With all the allure of a bad Scottish tourist café, it desperately needed help. It's typical of so many basements, but we knew just how to make it more comfortable, and far more welcoming.

Solution: C&J turn tartan tearaways—literally! We desperately needed to create a useable family rec room to provide our homeowners with valuable secondary living space when the house was overrun with grandchildren. We planned to create a new look with a whisper of Scotland but in a far more subtle way than before.

Before

Plus Points
* Adequate ceiling height for a basement
* Large rectangular room

Minus Points
* TV dominated the space
* Granny chic furniture that's more at home in the cottage
* Combo of wood panelling and tartan wallpaper—so 1970s!

After

With just the faintest whisper of the Scottish hills, this gorgeous room is now utterly transformed.

The stone wall provides instant atmosphere and is a textural feast that's really easy to install.

The material is essentially composed of large tiled sections, so the application is a job within the realms of most DIYers.

We mixed it up a little by opting for plaid fabric (the high chairs) and cream linen (the sofa) and then finished the look off with a leather armchair to anchor the entire new look.

Adding features adds personality. The warm wood tones of our new electric fireplace provide a wonderful focal point that helps you forget that this is actually a basement room!

The flat-screen TV is concealed in a now-you-see-it, now-you-don't rise and drop cabinet. Good design is all about problem solving, and today's marketplace has loads of interesting product to stash and conceal your technology. So get out there and get shopping!

Before

Sofas and Seating

BECAUSE MOST CANADIAN BASEMENTS ARE A little on the shallow side, we find it best to keep the lines of furnishings low slung to distract from vertically challenged rooms. Indeed, the lower your ceiling height, the more low slung should be your furniture. Opt for long lean sofas with a comfy squashy feel and seek out designs that have shorter legs to pull the eye down further.

By their very nature, family rooms are all about chilling out, so high-back "stand to attention" sofas (such as Queen Anne style or winged chesterfields) are not appropriate.

Keeping basement floor space as free as possible will allow for good circulation (and accommodating many family members at one time). You can increase your floor space by setting a sectional modular L-shaped sofa against one wall and placing a low-slung dual-purpose table (coffee table and storage chest, for example) in front. Position occasional tables at either end of the sofa, and add mood lighting to create a relaxed ambience.

Double-duty furniture, such as the coffee table mentioned above, can squeeze optimum flexibility from your family room. Look for tables that act as storage chests and storage cubes that moonlight as seating. Your space should be as multi-functional as possible, so incorporate surfaces where your children can do homework under close supervision while you catch up with your favourite TV show.

C&J'S TIP

Tastes change and what's hot one season can be not the next. We had been loathe to use beanbag chairs but we recently positioned not one but *three* massive beanbags in a rec room conversion and the results were fabulous. Our homeowners were nothing short of stunned when we suggested the squashy bags but were impressed by the results. It's all about context and being prepared to forgo apprehensions and try new (or is that old?) ideas!

Case Study: Little House on the Scary

Problem: Is it the mud room? Is it a laundry? Or is it the doghouse? Poor planning left this room suffering from acute multiple personality disorder. And as for that bile-green paint choice … even The Hulk would have winced!

Solution: Our plan was to create a zingy and well-equipped laundry room that would connect perfectly with the kitchen next door. The overall feel would be fresh and contemporary. We planned to install new appliances, piano-key tiling, and ceiling-mounted lighting. Serviceability and style in one easy package!

Before

Plus Points
* At least the room had a window!
* And a door that leads to the garden!

Minus Points
* Free-standing appliances that vibrate their way across the floor when in use
* Dog bed taking up space
* No counter space

After

With minimal spend for maximum impact, we completely transformed the room from its previously dull incarnation. Starting with the floor, we replaced the dirt-gathering fake slate tiles with easy-maintenance wood.

Positioning new appliances under the counter effectively pins them in and keeps them from wandering!

We installed a worktop to provide somewhere to sort and fold laundry. Little changes like this make for far greater efficiency. Don't we all want to feel like we've worked less?

Our brightly coloured tile detail at counter level provides visual design punctuation that brings the scheme to life, just like bright buttons on a plain suit.

A breakfast bar (formed from a spare piece of counter top) provides a handy spot to enjoy a coffee as the laundry spins!

Curtains and Window Treatments

ONE OF THE BIGGEST BASEMENT conundrums is how to make the very best of "problem" windows—you know the ones we mean. They're shallow, long, and skinny and positioned much nearer the ceiling (usually at ground level) than they would be in standard rooms. We've seen many half-baked problem-solving attempts so, in the name of good taste, here's our tried and tested method of window correction!

✳ First, extend the line of the existing window equally on each side.

✳ Then use wood frames to "fake out" a normal-sized window.

✳ Following the lines of any vertical or horizontal crossbars, fill in these sections with mirror to duplicate the size of the genuine glazing above.

✳ Hang floor-length curtains in the usual way. The long nature of the curtains will confuse the eye into "reading" a much taller wall height than actually exists!

Using the same principle, shutters would also be a useful problem solver.

C&J'S
Top 5 Tips to Make Your Basement Seem Deeper

Basements in many older houses do not have the same room heights as in other parts of the house. Digging down can be a solution. However, easier than full-scale excavation is to look at ways you can make your space seem deeper than it actually is. We have some C&J design tricks that will really help.

1 Paint ceilings in lighter tones than walls to effectively raise perceived head height.

2 Keep your ceiling lines as simple as possible by removing all crown moulding and cornices.

3 De-fuss by taking away picture rails and dado rails to stop your walls looking chopped up and therefore shorter.

4 Opt for narrower skirting boards painted in the same colour as walls to help them blend in.

5 Auspicious furniture selection will also help—as we showed in this chapter.

Take it from us—all these little design devices will conspire to make a big difference.

Studies and Offices

BUSINESS IS BOOMING—ON THE HOME FRONT, ANYWAY! WHEN IT COMES TO WORKING UNDER one's own roof, more and more people are doing it. What's more, as Canadians, you have more space per household than most of your European counterparts and more domestic square footage than many American homes. This is fabulous news if you want to set up a work environment *chez vous.*

Home businesses vary from those that can be set up in a corner of a room to those that need more space. Workshops and manufacturing studios are ideally located in larger environments such as garages, garden rooms, or basements, but more standard hives of industry can be located pretty much anywhere (in spare rooms or dens, for example) and, with creative planning, you should be able to find space in even the smallest home.

The fact of the matter is that most of us (whether running full-scale domestic-based commerce, bringing projects back from the office, or simply doing everyday home accounts) benefit from having a clearly demarcated space in which to work. More and more of us carry laptops, and many of us have fax machines and other office paraphernalia that need to be positioned carefully so they do not interfere with other aspects of your space. And when it comes to resale, space for a home office can add value to your home.

Locating Your Home Office

IT'S AMAZING WHAT YOU CAN ACHIEVE, SPATIALLY, IF YOU WORK HARD. Even if square footage is very limited, it's not the end of the world. We can help you open your eyes to the hidden space in your home. Those of you lucky enough to be able to dedicate a whole room to your office can skip this section ... or just enjoy the lovely pictures!

Find a Niche

While you may think there isn't space in your home, there are often nooks and crannies that can be successfully turned into workable space with a little imagination and designer jiggery-pokery.

Here's the very simplest solution: Create a workable nook by mounting a shelf on the top portion of a wall (to store files and other material) and positioning under it a wall-mounted fold-down table that can be raised or dropped as required. If you want to leave such a compact office set up permanently, use a screen to mask the corner. To further lessen the office impact, include a drawer in which your laptop can be stowed when not in use.

Space under the stairs or the landing between floors could be all you need to establish an efficient home office. Or perhaps your mud room could be given a dual purpose by replanning it to accommodate a desk, computer link, and seating. Bonus advantage: One minute you'll have an office chair, the next you'll have somewhere to sit as you undo your outdoor shoes or boots!

Out of the Closet

Do you have a large cupboard or closet that's stuffed with junk you no longer need or use? Have a garage sale and spend your windfall on "working up"

your new space! Walk-in cupboards can make great compact offices. Have your friendly handyman build a desktop (made of supporting wooden legs either side and a large flat section of particle board) in the closet and you'll instantly have a mini-space that will be the perfect escape from other aspects of home life. If there isn't already power inside the closet, have it wired to provide good overhead lighting and install a couple of electrical outlets—one above and one below your new desk counter— to provide power to your office equipment. Try to leave space below the desk to accommodate drawer storage—there's little point having a slick new office space and finding it immediately overrun with paper, files, and other office junk. Aye, a tidy office makes for a tidy mind!

Bedroom Business

A spare bedroom could be the very place to double as an office. If you still intend to host overnight guests, *completely* erasing hospitality space probably isn't the best idea. But if you can create a visibly "blurred" dual function by replacing an existing double bed with a sofa bed, your home office can still take shape—on a part-time basis when necessary. Simply pack up your office function when guests arrive and pull down that sofa bed to reveal comfy overnight sleeping accommodation.

The Business of Dining

It could even be that all you need to run an efficient home office is enough space at your dining table to position your laptop. The lightweight nature of today's portable computers (and their awesome data storage capacity) means it's now easy to dispense with that bulky old computer. If you set aside a couple of drawers in your sideboard, you can keep files and paperwork—as well as pens, pencils, and all manner of ancillary office stationery—out of sight.

Planning Your Home Office

NOW THAT YOU'VE WORKED OUT WHERE your home office is going to be, your next step is to consider how it's all going to work on a day-to-day basis. How much furniture can you comfortably squeeze in without congesting everything to such a point that it becomes uncomfortable? Is there enough room for a regular-sized desk or will space limitations dictate that you need to buy a smaller than standard width—or height—model?

For most people, maximizing the desk surface is important. Ensure that whatever you choose (whether custom construction or off the shelf) has space sufficient for good hand and arm ergonomics. Essentially this means there should be enough room for your wrists to have at least 6 inches of "sit space" in front of your keyboard and at least 24 inches either side for elbows to move up and down comfortably. Also check that your space allows for your legs to move comfortably under your desk without feeling tightly contained. Make sure there's enough room for filing cabinet or desk drawers to open properly, and that you can reach shelves or wall cabinetry without having to overstretch. You'll find it terribly constricting if your movement is limited by poor planning so work out proportions *before* going any further. If it doesn't look like everything is going to fit, go back to the drawing board and find another space in your home that will accommodate your needs.

Choosing Furniture

Don't be tempted to buy specialist office furniture just because you think you need furniture that looks like it belongs in an office. We think the best home office furniture doesn't *look* like regular office furniture. Instead of selecting a filing cabinet with a typically industrial aesthetic, consider a regular drawer set that has potential to be adapted as a storage spot for paper work. If you already have a small storage chest, look for compartmentalized filing systems to fit into it—not only are they easy to install, they also provide ample stash space for all your filing requirements. IKEA has a wonderful home office department, so head to the big blue and yellow shed for a world of inspiration!

Organizing Clutter

It's all too easy to let office paraphernalia run away with itself but doing so will ruin the productivity of your space. In addition, the paperless office just doesn't exist, in spite of the ubiquitous computer, which was touted to cut down on paper use. When we're putting together projects that include home offices, we always include discreetly positioned baskets, files, and drawers so every last detail can be organized. In larger offices, chests, sideboards, or credenzas can hide office supplies, office equipment, and piles of papers and files. An all-in-one printer—printer, fax machine, scanner—will help cut desktop clutter and cut down on the space you need. As far as we're concerned, a cluttered home office reflects clutter in other areas of your life. So keep it spic and span.

The Softening Effect

Remember to incorporate non-work-related aspects (such as family photos or objects with sentimental value) to ensure you feel centred and "personalized" in your office corner. If everything is too cold and clinical, it will have an effect on your output. If possible, try to locate your office space somewhere that has a window. A view toward the garden or a busy, friendly street will help you remain alert and focused and will allow the indulgence of a little daydreaming. Psychologists say a little escapism is valuable as a way of freeing up thought and prompting your imagination—traits that aren't encouraged by staring onto a blank wall!

Colour

WHILE DRAMATIC MOOD CAN BE COMFORTABLY ADDED IN certain home zones by opting for confident decorating, we'd recommend that in your home office you play things at a rather more *sedate* tempo. Even public-access internet cafés style their venues in a low-key—and never gaudily over-the-top—manner. For them it makes sense to keep visitors relaxed and subdued. With visitors paying by time, it's in the owner's interest to keep them focused on the job at hand and not propelled out the door courtesy of distracting decor. Which means everyone is happy—*you* get more work done and *they* get the revenue.

Working on a similar principle, we'd suggest creating a subtle background for your home office design. Almond shades, soft taupes, pale yellows, and light greens are organic tones that will relax you so your concentration remains fixed on your task. You can add colour via accessories. That said, don't make your office environment *too* plain. Keep your rooms stylish but remember that less is often more. Could be that all you need is a lovely piece of art to provide limited distraction or a strategically placed scatter cushion. Or perhaps a brightly coloured ceramic to add a little visual punch—and spot of visual relief—in an otherwise corporate (albeit domestic) world.

Case Study:
Bureau de Change!

After

Problem: Can you imagine anyone being able to work from this office? No, neither can we. Offices are supposed to be places of efficiency and order, something this room clearly knows nothing about!

Solution: Start filing and archiving before we even think about style!

Before

Plus Points

❋ Great potential
❋ House has huge basement ideal for archiving

Minus Points

❋ Anarchy!
❋ Office so cluttered, the work function had moved downstairs to the kitchen table!
❋ Tacky garage-style wall shelving

After

Don't incorporate negative elements into your new design—be ruthless and remove all that's bad before you start! Losing piles of rubbish, broken furniture, and decades of dust will provide a blank canvas upon which you can start. And remember, efficiency wins hands down, so dump all that's useless, archive older documents in the basement, and file all that's current close to hand.

Rather than leave great photographs and certificates rotting in boxes, we framed them

and hung them over the desk to create an achievement wall (not shown here), a visible reminder of just how fabulous this homeowner is.

Don't overstuff the home office—try to leave room to think. Too many items on the walls, congested furniture, and piles of clutter are distracting and not conducive to efficiency. Free your room, free your mind!

Because it's a home office, not an institution, you can soften the look with colour, cushions, and interesting flooring, as we did to friendly it up as much as possible.

Add a chair or two and your home office will stop being exclusively work-related and could in fact become somewhere to escape the family and read quietly!

Before

Window Dressings

IT'S ONE OF OUR REAL BUGBEARS, BUT HOME office window dressing is critically important for various reasons. In the first instance, the last thing you want is anyone peering in as you're getting on with work. And, from a design perspective, whatever you choose should complement your decorative scheme. We'd always advise you opt for a relatively uncomplicated look to help promote an "all business" feel.

If you have curtains you'd prefer stayed permanently open, you can position a simple roller blind out of sight at pelmet level—this shouldn't affect the overall look of your scheme as blinds can remain discreetly hidden when not in use. Come sunshine, however, they can be rolled down to block out glare. And don't automatically think you'll need to spend a fortune to play with natural light levels—these days most big box stores sell a fantastic range of blinds that won't break the bank.

C&J'S TIP

Ensure your window dressings are flexible enough to easily adjust the amount of light coming in. If you're using a computer, you'll find (even with the best anti-glare screens or removable light filters) that on even modestly sunny days the glare on your screen makes it almost impossible to see what you're typing. If you're constantly squinting and moving your screen so you can carry on working, that's a lot of wasted time that could be better spent getting on with the biz!

Case Study: Lose the Mess— Lose the Stress!

Problem: This home office is just way too dominant in its proximity to the living room, so it looks like a messy student bed-sit. Hey, even the ubiquitous student spider plant is present! Time for this place to graduate to the next level.

Solution: Design an office area sympathetic with the surroundings and discreet enough not to remind everyone of work!

Before

Plus Points
* Lots of natural light
* Generous space

Minus Points
* Very open onto living room
* Messy with papers piled around
* Dated, drab decor

After

If your office is in your living room, make it harmonious with the rest of your scheme. We replaced a faceless office desk with a period piece and immediately added loads of character. The big-footprint computer gave way to a laptop that fits into a drawer when not in use. Scanners, printers, and other unsightly items are stored in a nearby cupboard and accessed wirelessly.

The wall of mirrors looked like a dated fitted wardrobe, but we had to admit that their reflective nature made the room feel larger, so we devised a plan to update rather than reject. Our solution was to frame the wall to look like three individual mirrors. We glued inexpensive

4 x 1 pine to the surface, matching the wood tone to the desk to provide visual continuity.

In mixed-use areas and open-plan rooms, spell out exactly where one function ends and another begins. Using area rugs is an age-old designer trick to reinforce space as well as soften a hard-floored room. The chocolate tones of this sisal rug tie in perfectly with the wood of the floor.

The lighting comes from three sources that can be used independently or combined to create a variety of effects. Overheads illuminate the space, a floor lamp provides for comfy chair reading, and a desk lamp lights the work surface.

In open-plan spaces, try to get double duty from each item. Look for desks that become drinks cabinets, chairs that swing round to service two areas, or an ottoman that serves as storage *and* extra seating.

Before

Lighting

SETTING ATMOSPHERE VIA LIGHTING IS important in any room, not least in the office at home. Too much glare and you'll feel distracted, but, conversely, too little light and your work space will feel dull. We like to combine task and mood lighting so we generally recommend adding a desktop lamp (preferably one with an adjustable arm that can be twisted and directed as required) and sufficient overhead lighting to create perfect balance. Don't forget to install one of our tried and tested instant mood fixers—the good old Canadian dimmer switch. Twenty bucks' worth of hardware will offer brilliant light level flexibility.

C&J'S
Top 8 Home Office Tips

1 **Get rid!** Don't keep every scrap of correspondence that enters your home. Be vigilant about recycling, and retain only that which you actually need. Wherever possible, try to run a paper-free office and consign what you can to (backed-up) computer files. Even in a large busy home, all relevant household bills can be kept in a small log. In the same way that you consign out-of-season garb to the basement till needed again, file away paperwork that you need to keep but perhaps don't need to access on a regular basis. For everything else, into the recycling bin or paper shredder with it!

2 **Unify!** It's amazing how easy it is to unify mismatched office furniture with a coat of paint or a few even applications of spray varnish. Coordinating in this way can create wonderfully streamlined effects. But remember: Don't rush things; a few light coats (with ample drying time between each) are always better than one sticky gloopy application.

3 **Go wireless ...** Even modest economic outlays can reap big rewards. Reduce that dangerous tangle of trip-hazard wiring and tidy up!

4 **... and hide remaining hardware.** Machinery such as printer, fax, and photocopier can be easily stashed behind closed doors to further free up counter space. A reworked living room hutch or armoire can be compartmentalized to house an astonishing amount of office kit—not to mention all the paperwork that you need to keep close at hand.

5 **Keep it light.** Leave the dreary colours that typify corporate business to … the corporate world. Forget that dusty palette of dark shades and gloomy mahogany. And, while you're at it, ditch the green and burgundy leather that typifies the 70s and 80s. Instead, choose a scheme that's light and fresh so your office wakes you up rather than sending you off to a land of dull decor dozing!

6 **Balance the budget.** You don't have to employ a master carpenter—or a specialist office outfitter—to create a solid and workable home office environment. Careful selection of budget furniture and using second-hand adaptable items will help create the perfect space while leaving you with spare funds for accessories. Which is *always* good news!

7 **Remember the comfort factor.** If space permits, try to incorporate some elements of soft furnishing so you can treat yourself to a little relaxation between bouts of productivity! And remember—one good sofa or chaise is generally much better than a squashed-in selection of chairs and stools. Office seating is not meant for socializing sessions, so bear this in mind as you make your selections.

8 **Keep your dramatic predilections in tow and follow fashion—with care.** Some interior decorating mags may have told you to follow the runway trends of Paris and Milan. We, however, while not shy to include fashion in the home, would always counsel that you take it easy. It's simple (and less expensive) to change your clothes on a whim, but just try changing your interior as soon as a magazine editor tells you that red is suddenly the new black. You could just find yourself scuppered and living in a space that makes you feel decidedly last season!

Office space no-nos!

Bathrooms

FOR SOME PEOPLE, THE BATHROOM IS LITTLE MORE THAN AN AFTERTHOUGHT AND simply a place where washing and other essential matters take place. However, we're thrilled to report there's been a serious flush (if you'll excuse the pun) of interest in this potentially wonderful domestic zone. The importance of the bathroom should never be underestimated, and we consider its potential as the great human rejuvenator to be huge. In days gone by, bathrooms were very much a case of "in and out" and "wash and go," yet today the bathroom is evolving into a spa at home. Indeed, we often wonder why people pay to dash off to exclusive—and expensive—health resorts when the home spa can so easily be shaped to give a wonderful return without stepping out of the front door!

We have also noticed from literally hundreds of visits to clients' homes that the new holy grail fantasy is to squeeze in as many bathrooms as possible. In our experience, Canadians have more bathrooms per house than their British counterparts, so we recognize that you guys have been blazing the trail for indulgent cleansing for longer than others!

Our Credo

BEFORE WE GO ANY FURTHER, WE HAVE TO clearly state our fundamental bathroom rule: Bathroom suites can be any colour as long as they're white!

That means your avocado suite—or your powder pink suite for that matter—has simply got to go! But don't panic—these days, refitting has become more affordable as bathroom hardware prices have plunged due to a highly competitive market. It's now possible to pick up a brand-new full-depth white soaker tub (and who doesn't want a fabulous soaker tub!) and matching white sink and toilet set from around $600. Even if you factor in another few hundred dollars for a plumber (and some bargain basement white tiles) you can have a great bathroom reno for around a thousand bucks. Oh, and did we say … everything's white, of course.

The Perfect Bathroom

ALL BATHROOMS NEED TO HAVE THE BASICS: A TOILET, a sink, and a bathtub or shower. From there, you can add whatever your heart desires, your budget allows, and just as important, whatever your space will accommodate.

As you assess your needs, remember that it's essential your bathroom design be as simple as possible because, just like the kitchen, it is anchored by built-in elements that are hard to change. It's not like the bedroom or the living room, where you can tailor the mood to the moment with a few carefully selected accessories. With this in mind, it's crucial to get the balance right from the start and to plan your direction accordingly.

How You Use Your Bathroom

Every makeover starts with the fundamental issue of how the room is to be used. The bathroom is no different. It is essential to spend time analyzing what your room needs to give you and how it needs to function. If you have more than one bathroom in your house, first appraise what you hope to achieve with each space. Who uses which bathrooms? If you have only one, how many people need to use it for bathing, shaving, primping, and the other things for which bathrooms are used? Would it make sense to separate some of these functions if at all possible—could you set the toilet and a small sink in a room of its own, leaving the remaining space

Case Study:
Basement Bathroom

After

Problem: The retired couple who own this house positively brimmed with life but their basement spare room was little more than dead space. However, we had a plan.

Solution: Reclaim dead, wasted space and rebirth it all as something thoroughly worthwhile and extravagant. All hail the spa bathroom, C&J style!

Before

Plus Points
* Basement has excellent ceiling height
* Room has window

Minus Point
* No plumbing in place

After

We added a classic chrome-framed vanity to breathe breeding and quality into our bathroom design. Chrome taps, slate tiling, and bales of fluffy towels complete the hedonistic look!

There's no point scrimping on the soak factor so indulge yourself with a large deep tub. And take a tip: Don't be afraid to try your choice out for size (and comfort) in the showroom. Though at this stage you should really keep your clothes on!

Don't feel you have to be regimented when it comes to tiling—mixing different sizes will add interest, though wherever possible, try to match up lines and edges where tiles meet.

We created mirrored storage towers on either side of the bath to showcase all manner of lovely things, and we also made use of the space either side as handy towel storage.

Remember to titillate your olfactory senses! Indulge in gorgeous scented candles (but don't leave them unattended) and pack shelves with essential oils poured into decorative jars and bottles. And, to promote optimum relaxation, fit a dimmer switch to change the mood at the twist of a button!

Before

for bathing or showering, putting on makeup, and checking your weight every morning?

If you have a bathroom used by all members of the household and an ensuite in the master bedroom, it might make sense to think about whether you really need to have a bathtub in both rooms or a shower in both. If you love bathing, surely it's best to have a luxurious tub (complete with power jets and all manner of bells and smells) in one room rather than narrow shallow tubs in both rooms. And are you really likely to use that bidet or could everything be rejigged in a more effective way without it? Perhaps the floor space could be better used as

a cupboard or display storage for all your lovely bathroom accessories.

The Space Race

Bathrooms were traditionally the smallest rooms in most homes—not surprising, as they were there simply as functional rooms. Today, however, many homeowners want luxury in the bathroom. So, with this in mind, you're going to have to use some clever tricks to make it appear that proportions are more generous than they are. Here are a few tried and true design tricks we've used—feel free to adapt them to your own needs!

* Mirror an entire wall.

* An even easier device is to use a metallic-finish wallpaper or even satin finish (rather than matte) latex paint to help bounce light around.

* Use shiny tiles or stainless steel finishes to add "perceived magnification."

* Sometimes scaling down to a slightly smaller bath will mean that everything fits in. This is a last resort for us because we firmly believe that a cramped tub is an unhappy tub! Before we go for this option, we jiggle the layouts a bit or move bathing to another room as a better alternative.

C&J'S TIP

An unused bedroom can be developed into a stunning spa at home or even an exciting shower or wet room (though the latter needs extra-special planning and a high degree of waterproofing to protect the floor and rooms below). Such transformations create a valuable asset that will be enjoyed more by you and the family than had it remained an occasionally used guest bedroom. However, if you are planning to sell your property in the near future, losing a bedroom is probably not a good idea—more bedrooms often equal more bucks.

During the massive *Home Heist* refurbishment of Cathie's bathroom, we banished the bidet and created this wonderfully indulgent zone instead. Gorgeous, huh?

Case Study:
Two Become One

Problem: A two-bedroom house with two tiny washrooms sitting unhappily side by side—if you're the builder of this home, could you write in and tell us why?

Solution: We created a spacious bathroom that's thoroughly in keeping with the cottage charm of the rest of the house.

Before

Plus Points

* At least one WC was in the right place
* Wall between both rooms was plaster board and not load-bearing

Minus Points

* Both rooms were cramped
* No windows
* Dated and dull design

After

Quality over quantity—we knocked two bad rooms into one great space to create a gorgeous new bathroom. By leaving the bath and one of the toilets in the original spots, we were able to keep costs down.

A bathroom should make you feel fresh and clean before you've even turned on a tap, so choose colours that promote a bright feeling. This is especially important if your bathroom is an internal room without natural light.

We laid black-and-white floor tiles in a checkerboard style to hark back to the art deco period—classically stylish and surprisingly good value!

We opted for a leggy vanity unit with towel rail instead of a more solid unit to keep the room feeling spacious—the chrome ties in with taps, handles, and rails.

Mirror finishes bounce light around and make this compact room feel much larger than it actually is. If you have space, add a small table or chair to create another layer of interest in your bathroom.

We positioned wall sconces on either side of the mirror to illuminate the face without creating shadows—overhead ceiling lighting can leave you looking less than your best when shaving or applying makeup.

We added tongue-and-grove wood wall panelling to half-height to extend the cottage feel and add further visual interest.

Hardware

HERE'S OUR SECOND BATHROOM RULE: Endeavour to make fixed elements as low key as possible. You've watched our shows so you know what we mean. You've never seen us install anything other than simple, elegant fixtures, generally flat-sided baths as opposed to bow-fronted options. These bow-fronted tubs don't have "box-in panel" potential and therefore can never have a new tile front added as decorative tastes change. Something else you've *never* seen us do: install a corner bath! It's all about keeping to simple lines that can be the basis for further decorative elements. The fanciest we ever get is when we choose a roll-top vintage bath with elegant lion's claw feet or one that's set on funky timber blocks. Where we will add the extras, however, is with luxury features that don't interfere with the overall visual. So that means yes to baths with built-in massage jets, yes to heated towel rails, yes to indulgent shower stalls, and even yes to the odd bit of bathroom-proof sound and vision equipment.

Paint and Painted Surfaces

IN RECENT YEARS, THE PAINT INDUSTRY HAS MADE marvellous strides in creating paints with greatly improved durability. A paint that is resistant to water is extremely important in the bathroom (and also in the kitchen). The bathroom is the room that's most susceptible to damp due to moisture that is constantly in the atmosphere. These "smart" moisture-repellent paints inhibit the production of mould and are more easily maintained than standard paint. And the even better news is that while these paints were often available only in white (or perhaps "daring" bathroom blue), they're now available in an inspired range of shades that will help bring new drama to your space. Refer to our colour chapter on page 266 for more on choosing colours.

Adding to the Comfort Factor

WHEN YOU'RE WORKING OUT A PLAN FOR where sanitary wares will go, it's worth trying to eke out some spare space for loose furniture such as a chair or perhaps even a free-standing cabinet that can double as display for such things as bales of fluffy towels or jars of gorgeous bath oils. All the better if you can fit in a full-length mirror. It can do double duty, giving you somewhere to check your look and also helping bounce light around to increase the feeling of roominess.

Built-in shelving, too, is an element that's often overlooked when designing bathrooms, although we make it one of the primary elements to which we attend as soon as we're in front of our drawing boards. If you're fitting shelving, make some of them with doors—that way you can stash away all the bathroom paraphernalia you'd rather stayed hidden!

We've found that thinking outside the box can pay *fabulous* dividends, especially when it comes to cabinetry. Rather than consulting only specialist bathroom fitters, also speak to kitchen suppliers who may be able to custom-tailor less expensive cabinetry to suit your purposes. Just because something was designed for one room doesn't mean it can't be useful in another! In our experience, the range of colours and finishes available for kitchen cabinetry is far in advance of those offered by bathroom suppliers. Cabinets designed for kitchens need to be hard-wearing and will stand up equally to the demands of the bathroom.

C&J'S TIP

Squeeze out extra function from overlooked corners. Here are a couple of ideas:

• Use clever carpentry around your traditional pedestal sink to provide an additional vanity surface as well as great door-fronted storage below.

• Carefully consider the placement of hardware such as bath, sink, and toilet. If you have a long skinny bathroom, try positioning your bath along one wall. At the end that faces you as you walk into the room, build a ceiling-height wall the width of the bath and add chunky drywall shelving.

Case Study:
Bad Taste, No Taste

Problem: The sun should have set long ago on this scary sun-moon-and-stars-themed bathroom. Check out the tiles, the bathroom suite, and the plastic bag–lined bin next to the loo. It's enough to make you hurl.

Solution: We designed a bathroom that feels spacious and efficient, a luxurious wash zone that's conducive to rest and relaxation.

Before

Plus Points

* Is there even one positive thing to say about this crime scene? *Ahem*, no!

Minus Points

* Dark walls and shoddy shower curtain make for a cramped feeling
* Dated design with gloomy overtones
* Outsized vanity unit consumed loads of floor space but housed only one sink
* Coloured bathroom suite? Last fashionable when Moses was still a boy …

After

Limestone tiling looks expensive, and that's probably because it can be! But hey, with results this good, it's well worth investing. We used the same tile style from floor to ceiling to simplify and enlarge the tight space.

If you crave colour, add it via tiles, window treatments, artwork, and accessories.

Rather than hang a shower curtain, we used clear glass panels to add understated wow factor. Doing this made the bathroom feel larger as the screen is effectively invisible. What's more, our owners won't ever get that slightly damp

smell that can happen with a past-its-best curtain. Specialist glaziers can easily tackle this project or you might be lucky enough to find something in your size off the shelf.

We removed the sink, swung the bath over across the width of the room, and moved the toilet forward to create a much more usable plan. Next, we positioned a new sink—opposite the toilet—for a balanced look. If you're installing a new bathroom, look at different layout options rather than simply repeating what's gone before.

The dark wood vanity unit warms up the room and brings a natural element that we continued via accessories such as the towel storage bins.

Mix styles to add interest. We used a chunky ornate mirror to provide contrast to flat, smooth walls and to give our finished design an air of quality.

Before

Bathroom Lighting

NATURAL LIGHT IS IMPORTANT IN ANY ROOM but in a bathroom it seems even more critical. It's a space dedicated to cleanliness so it should feel bright and hygienic at all times, and good lighting will help promote this feeling. If your bathroom doesn't have a window, there are several ways of introducing natural light—for example, by installing fanlights, also known as transom windows, over the door so light can bleed in from the hallway. If you're on the top floor, you could consider installing a skylight, although for this we'd recommend talking to the local planning department. Sometimes the only solution is a spread of overhead spotlights to lighten things up. One clever way of introducing natural light is through a device called a Solatube. We've added these in a couple of houses and they really do make a difference. However, because they are installed inside the walls, you need the space to bring them down through the wall cavity. They work by bouncing light from mirror to mirror as the tube curves its way down the building wall.

C&J'S TIP

If you're illuminating a mirror, it's better to have lights on either side of it (rather than above)—overhead lighting casts difficult and unflattering shadows, making applying make-up or shaving a great deal harder.

On previous projects, where clients have been particularly keen on having something that at least looks like a window, we created frosted backlit panels in the shape and size of a standard window, then positioned faux framework and cross beams to create the illusion of the real thing. We've even gone to the extent of hanging curtains or a blind to build the image of the real thing even further!

Flooring and Wall Tile

INVARIABLY, WE GO FOR CERAMIC, STONE, OR granite in the bathroom, on both walls and floor. Tiles lend an air of sophistication to the bathroom and, on a more practical level, they are easy to keep clean in a room that should be synonymous with hygiene.

Walking into a tile shop can be an overwhelming experience, as choices seem endless—which colour or colours should you choose, shiny or matte finish, and which shapes and sizes? Our advice, generally, is to go for a neutral colour so that you have an accommodating base against which you can redecorate and change the colour scheme as your tastes and fashion change. We do break the rule now and then, though—check out George and Margaret's bathroom (left) after our transformation.

One complaint we hear about tile floors is that they are cold. In a hot Canadian summer, that's no problem! But in a chilly winter, you don't want to shock your tootsies. One solution is under-floor heating. If this is the option you choose, you need to plan ahead for its installation. If you're looking for a less expensive solution, try a colourful scatter rug in front of the vanity so you don't get the chills while shaving or brushing your teeth. As you know, we hate carpet in the bathroom, but at least you can sling the mat through the washer! (And, as a last resort, how about wearing slippers?)

For George and Margaret, we really went to town and created a totally hedonistic bathroom that was a paradise of tonal graphite shades. Over the top? Well, we loved it, but more importantly, so did our happy couple.

Case Study:
No Shagging in the Bathroom

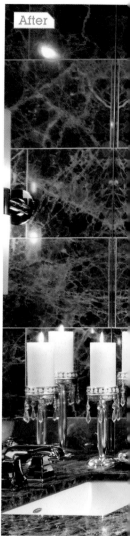

Problem: Check out the shag carpet wrapped around this 1970s relic bathroom! *Noooooooooo!* And what about the doll house–style vanity unit, the awful wall tiles, and the colour of that suite? All in all, a dated time warp disaster!

Solution: We created a classic family bathroom with an indulgent air of opulence more in keeping with this well-kept (if rather dated) Italian family home.

Before

Plus Points

* Spotlessly clean room that had been lovingly appreciated for decades!
* Large square footage

Minus Points

* Too much wasted space
* Oversized tub—and its surround—dominated the room
* Shag carpeting everywhere—not so groovy, baby!

After

Bathrooms aren't just about bathing, they're important worlds where you can escape the stresses of daily life, zones to indulge and generally rejuvenate. Here, we ticked all the boxes with double sinks for two-person tooth brushing, a walk-in shower for fast turnaround, and a huge soaker tub for a long, languid bath.

We were inspired by the Amalfi Coast and the grandeur of traditional five-star hotels. An all-round finish like this floor-to-ceiling toffee marble tile not only looks fantastic but is also amazingly easy to keep clean. Yes, genuine marble is pricey, but it's well worth investing in to create a timeless look. And just think of the added value come sales time!

The shower has an almost invisible appearance thanks to the straight lines of the clear glass box that forms the cubicle. Clear glass increases the feeling of space and adds to the sense of cleanliness. And don't panic too much about cost—even big-box stores now carry off-the-shelf enclosures for a fraction of the price of custom installation.

We obscured the toilet with a modesty wall/ storage tower built from fibreboard tiled to match the walls. We created towel and toiletry storage pockets and even installed a flat-screen TV to enjoy while soaking in the tub! Visible-spend items like taps and light fittings add to the feeling of luxury.

Heating

BECAUSE BATHROOMS ARE USUALLY ON THE compact side, it makes sense to keep heating hardware as small as possible so you don't impinge on valuable space. Wall-mounted heaters are great solutions, but make sure they're positioned so they don't interfere as you move around your bathroom—it'll be a real problem, after all, if you're forever burning your legs when you step out of the bath.

Another possibility is boxing in a radiator with a decorative vented panel, ensuring, of course, that there's sufficient air passage around it. Consider installing a heated towel ladder, a device that's long been popular in Britain but is now more readily available in Canada too. With these you get a double benefit—effective heating and somewhere to store and dry towels. These rails can be mounted well off the floor so little fingers won't get burned—the railings can get quite warm.

Our favourite way of keeping the bathroom cozy is by installing under-floor heating, though be warned that this is a job best tackled when your space is being completely overhauled—it's quite an invasive undertaking and involves laying a heating element (as the name suggests!) under tile or, in some cases, wood. As usual, we'd recommend talking to your retailer to check product specs and the suitability of this solution for your project.

C&J'S
Top 5 Ways to Make Your Bathroom Look More Expensive

1. If you want a whisper of marble, limestone, or granite—but without the big spend of a full fit-out—complement your favourite stone with tonally similar budget tiles used as trim around mirrors or at half-height up walls, with a border of genuine stone.

2. In the same way that coordinated jewellery (earrings, necklace, and bracelets, for example) can dress up a basic suit, so too can a sequence of matching accessories (chrome towel rail, toilet roll holder, and soap dish) create the illusion that lots of cash has been invested.

3. New taps can update a basic white suite. A few extra dollars spent will make all the difference and will really help set a luxurious scene.

4. Get rid of the clutter—a messy space looks uncared for and presents entirely the wrong image. A tidy bathroom is a happy bathroom!

5. Lose all those sticky half-empty bottles and jars and replace them with attractive vases full of essential oils and potions. And, while you're at it, stock up on masses of fluffy towels—but don't hide them away in a cupboard. Display them on shelves or in pretty baskets.

Hallways

HERE'S ONE OF THE MOST RELEVANT MAXIMS IN HOME STYLING AND interior design circles: You only get one chance to make a first impression. And your hall—or entranceway—is where that impression starts. Indeed, from the moment people enter your world they are, whether you like it or not, making judgments about your space that will be difficult to change even if the rest of your rooms are in fabulous order. Nothing, after all, says neglected more than flaky paint, peeling wallpaper, or curled-up carpet (all of which have featured regularly in many of the hallways we've seen), so get it right, from the start!

In our view, hallways are much more than passageways to other rooms. They are the style setters for what lies beyond and important spaces in their own right. Dress them correctly and they'll make you and your visitors feel energized and welcome. And the best news? Making a commanding opening statement doesn't need to be difficult or, for that matter, expensive. Here's how …

The Face of the House

THE FRONT OF THE HOUSE IS LIKE A PERSON'S face—it can be welcoming, warm, and friendly or it can be grumpy, untidy, and unfriendly. If you approach dressing the front of your house with the same care you take when you apply makeup or trim your moustache, you'll be presenting the best face you can to visitors, neighbours, and passersby. Although a face has certain common elements—a nose, two eyes, a mouth, a chin—the front of a house can vary greatly. Sometimes the main entry is not even at the front of the house. But no matter where it is, that entry to the house is important.

Front Doors

Often the first thing a visitor is exposed to is your front door. The best colours for front doors traditionally have been Oxford blue, white, deep green, deep red, or black. These are strong, bold, no-nonsense colours. Where there aren't any restrictions that stipulate what can or can't be done, such as you might find in condo blocks or shared ownerships, we colour our portals with one of these shades. The front door of our Glasgow Georgian home, for example, is painted dramatic satin black and features stainless steel door furnishings that makes a low-key yet confident statement. In our 1930s London apartment we've opted for glossy white and dressed it with a brass letter box and an art deco knob and number set. It's important to respect the period of build but, generally, we

always comes back to one of our five favoured shades for front doors, storm doors, or screens. Survey after survey has shown these colours to be consistently popular with buyers and sellers alike.

Other Outdoor Elements

Lights

There's little more frustrating than a poorly lit entranceway, so brighten up, guys, before going any further with your design! We always recommend installing a motion sensor light outside a front door. Position so it spreads light directly from above to provide helpful illumination when you need it most. Not only will it be useful as you fumble in your pocket or purse for your keys but it'll also be invaluable as you look from inside at anyone who's just knocked at your door.

Mats

We have taken to positioning a door mat in front of every project we work on. You'd be surprised just how much dirt and debris is trailed inside from unwiped shoes and boots. The best door mats have a deep bristled pile and are generally black, dark green, brown, or sand coloured.

C&J'S TIP

Many Canadian homes have mud rooms or entry closets, which are not as common in Britain. We've come to love mud rooms because you can kiss goodbye to outdoor footwear before entering the main part of your home. We've pledged that for any new homes we build (in Canada, Britain, or beyond) we'll be including mud rooms—a great addition if your home doesn't already have one.

Case Study:
Perfect But Ugly

Problem: Well, talk about a less-than-warm welcome! Not only is this one of the gloomiest hallways in Canada, it also has a rather dangerous highly polished tiled floor that even Wayne Gretzky would find too slippery … and as for the ornamental guard dog—woof woof!

Solution: Create a design that is fresh and modern and able to frame the elegant staircase.

Before

Plus Points

* Grand hallway and staircase
* Lots of natural light

Minus Points

* Too open to kitchen/dining area
* Dated lighting
* Dangerous flooring
* Tacky dog ornament

After

We love open-concept living, but having the dining kitchen open to the front door was a step too far, especially in this very large home. We added glass doors to foreshorten the hallway but still allow natural daylight to pass through.

The pattern on the wall was created by masking off stripes with tape and then painting bands in two shades of grey. The vertical bands lift the ceiling height and provide smart and elegant detailing.

Treat hallways like proper rooms and add furniture to provide purpose—you'll feel like you've gained another room! Here, a simple dresser acts as an anchor piece above which a framed piece of art can be hung. This gives the room a focal point, which in turn makes it easier to dress.

Previously, an abundance of hanging shades were competing with each other for attention. We swapped the lower fittings for pot lights set flush in the ceiling and kept the fitting in the centre of the staircase as our focal lamp. The black chandelier fits in well with the grey decor and ties in beautifully with the black handrail and carpet edging strip.

We lost the highly polished ice-rink tiled floor in favour of wood-effect vinyl boards that bring natural warmth into the design while still being easy to clean and warm underfoot. The floor adds to the overall appearance of quality in the hallway and works well with the painted plaster wall detail.

Designing the Hallway

WHEN DESIGNING A HALLWAY, THINK ABOUT the space as an important part of your home. Creating a welcoming feeling will win you design points every time so make your hallway lavish, as if it were somewhere you might actually want to spend some time, rather than seeing it simply as the zone that links other rooms in your home. Let's start with what's underfoot.

Flooring

Whenever we can (and budget permitting), we'll specify solid wood flooring at the point of entry. From a maintenance perspective, it's one of the most serviceable options of all as long as it's regularly cleaned of soil and debris. Other choices, such as Karndean or Amtico, which look like wood, tile, or stone, make for superb flooring. Ceramic or stone tiles are also sensible hallway options but keep in mind what will work best for your situation. If you do use tile or stone, consider using an under-floor heating membrane, which will take the edge off the cold factor that's often associated with this type of flooring. These elements have to be installed *before* the floor is laid but they represent great value and are pretty much maintenance-free.

Carpets are a serviceable option as long as you choose a product with high or entire man-made content. If properly looked after, they will repel dirt and stand up to the rigours of heavy domestic traffic. Seagrasses and similar natural fibres are harder to clean due to their more porous nature. In a big hallway, large area rugs will visually warm the space—this is true no matter the room's purpose as layers always make everything look very considered and thoughtful.

No matter which type of flooring you choose for the entryway and hallway, the criteria are the same: it should be serviceable; it should be washable; and it should be able to cope with wear and tear.

Walls

Hallways get a lot of traffic—they're the connection to most of the rooms in the house. As a result, there's loads of opportunity for hallway walls to become scratched, scraped, or damaged by furniture coming in and out, or simply by human traffic. Because of this, we ensure that wall coverings in our hallways are hard-wearing and sturdy enough to cope. In the inner areas of the hallway, where doors can swing onto surfaces, we avoid wallpaper and generally choose washable paint that can be scrubbed down or repainted as required. And we're not too shy to perform the old hotel trick of installing pre-measured clear acrylic sheeting to act as a protector, particularly at vulnerable points where damage is most likely.

Colour Scheming

To make your hall as welcoming as possible, paint it in a warm tone that immediately settles

C&J'S TIP

As an extra safeguard, we generally position a bristle "drop-in" or mat that fits into a recess in the floor. It will catch any debris that has managed to make it past the front door mat. The product you choose should have a similar depth to your main flooring. If the bristle pile is too long, you can inadvertently create a trip hazard.

you as soon as you walk in the door. Because space is often limited, select "enlarging" colours—creams, taupes, and soft shades such as yellow or palest blue. In larger halls, look at a more spirited shade such as terracotta or warm green to create a welcoming feel. If you're keen to use colour but are concerned about scale, custom mirroring a section of one wall or simply hanging a large shop-bought framed mirror will help bounce light around and help balance out a darker tone in a smaller space.

Cleverly chosen paint can be used to change the perceived scale in any room, but it's in the hallway that some of the most useful tricks can be played. Hall problems are fairly similar and we have tried and true ways of addressing and fixing these issues. Here are a few classic C&J solutions you should find helpful.

✴ **Bring down the ceiling height in a tall skinny hallway.** If you have scale issues because of a top-heavy narrow space, install a picture rail and paint the space above it in a shade two or three tones darker than your main wall areas. Doing this will instantly make the ceiling height seem to drop and your space will feel much more manageable.

✴ **Make a long hall seem shorter or a skinny hall wider.** If your hall feels more like a never-ending train tunnel than a welcoming entry to your home, paint the end wall a few shades darker than the side walls. Doing this will provide a subtle design keynote, but more importantly, it will also effectively "pull" the far wall nearer, creating the impression that your passageway is shorter than it actually is. It's a simple trick, but it works every time!

✴ **Cozy up a large hall.** Here's an old trick you may have spotted in restaurants that don't have vestibules: a thick curtain dressed against the front door. It does more than make the space feel warmer. It also adds visual depth and makes everything look more luxurious into the bargain.

To make this work, either hang the curtain from a rail fixed to the top of the door or employ a hoop rail to create an intimate circular "ante area."

Hall Harmony

We use the term "design transition" to describe a way by which to ensure your hallway has a relationship with the other spaces into which it leads. Some examples will help explain what we mean by this term. If you have a warm decorative scheme in your living room that uses, say, red and gold, using some of the elements of the same colour scheme in the hallway will tie the two areas together in a subtle but effective way. We're not suggesting you copy decorative elements exactly, but linking, with key schematic aspects such as colour, is a very sensible principle.

Perhaps your living room has a blue feature wall, as well as navy upholstery and other "softs" used lavishly. It could be that the only thing required to join it to your hallway is a large cobalt blue ceramic drum (perhaps to hold brollies?) or a proudly displayed dramatic blue glass vase. These tiny details may not be consciously noted by your visitors, but the impression will be one of luxury and harmony.

Lighting

We've already talked about the light that welcomes guests outside, but we also recommend a directional pot light be positioned inside, above your front door, to continue the warm welcome as your guests walk inside. Make

C&J'S TIP

Don't get carried away with installing too many pot lights or your ceiling will end up looking like an airport runway. Ensure that each pot has a function, either to provide general illumination or to pinpoint artwork or objects displayed on a console table to dramatic effect.

sure the switch for this light is in an easy-to-reach spot—and not behind ladders, stacks of boxes, or mounds of coats! Generally, if hallway proportions are narrow, we'll also install a line of pots to provide sufficient full hall illumination and, as usual, one of our beloved dimmer switches to adjust levels as required.

If proportions are generous, and your hallway can cope with a pendant light, your options are limitless. Fittings can be chosen to provide dramatic punctuation in otherwise neutral spaces. And don't forget that the shape of the fitting can also be used to play with perceived space. If your ceilings are low, choose fittings that are shallow, and conversely, if your ceilings are high and you'd like to "fill" the overhead space, select shades or chandeliers that are generously deep.

C&J'S
Top 6 Tips to Make Your Hallway Welcoming

1 **Keep hallways clear of unnecessary clutter.** Hang a couple of coats in your hallway but edit those that are not being used on a daily basis—store them in closets until they're genuinely needed.

2 **Ditch the free sheets!** Have you allowed weeks of supermarket flyers and local rags to build into wayward piles of space-consuming junk? Pitch it all in the recycling bin and, immediately after that, hang a "no junk mail" sign on your door to deter future overzealous advertisers. While you're at it, if you have a letter box that's a slot in the door, position a basket inside to catch mail so your hungry dog doesn't eat it all before you can grab it!

3 **Hang artwork.** If wall space permits, hang artwork in the hall, so it feels like a valuable part of your home.

4 **Position a mirror for a final checkup.** This is a no-brainer. Just as you're charging out the door, it's useful to have somewhere to check your look. And while you're at it, pop a handy shelf below it to stash keys.

5 **Light up a gloomy hall by choosing glazed internal doors.** If the openings to the rooms off the hall have doors, opt for door designs and constructions that complement your overall scheme and period of build. If they have glass panels, they will bleed light from the other rooms into the hall, which will enlarge and brighten it.

6 **Use furniture in the hall.** We hate to see an area going to waste when it could potentially be "dressed"! That's why we always fit in a chair or a small table if space permits.

Porches and Decks

AS WE TRAVEL CANADA ON OUR ENTERTAINING, IF SOMEWHAT RELENTLESS, mission of decorative beautification, we're constantly inspired by an army of outdoors devotees and by the work they've done to ensure porches and decks (not to mention patios and terraces!) are as fabulous as possible. We're thrilled to see a growing commitment to improving exterior space and, as two devoted fans of alfresco entertainment, we can only imagine the fun and hospitality that takes place. We *love* seeing the best being made of homes both inside and out. We recently even cut the ribbon at Canada Blooms, one of North America's largest celebration of all things pertaining to the outdoors. Which was fabulously convenient as we're currently working on the transformation of our own Toronto roof terrace, which, at thirty-nine floors up, faces all manner of assault from Canada's climate. But that's another story …

Porches

THE PORCH IS YOUR CHANCE TO MAKE A good impression on passersby and visitors. It is the welcoming—or off-putting—face of your house and the only visual clue people have as to who you are—do you take pride in your home? Are you sloppy and careless? Friendly? Unfriendly? Yes, the public exterior of your home tells a tale—and often perhaps more than you'd like!

Making a Good First Impression

What is the purpose of a porch? This, to us, is a no-brainer. A porch should serve as a welcoming stop-off point as you search for your keys. It should provide visitors with somewhere to wait, sheltered from the elements, as you make your way to greet them. Porches also allow you to spend time outdoors even if the weather is bad and, if properly shielded from winds via roll-down all-weather blinds or vinyl screening, they can even be enjoyed into the autumn. Add a (supervised) patio heater and you could even find yourself savouring a mug of alfresco hot chocolate as winter takes hold!

Porches that wrap above windows also help shield your home from the heavy glare of sunlight and, as well as protecting your eyes while indoors, they can deflect sunlight so your furniture doesn't become faded and bleached over time. As well as all this, auspiciously positioned porches will help protect the external walls of your home from water ingress via rain or snow coursing down the roof.

In spite of these aesthetic and practical advantages, all too often we've found neglected porches and decks, even when there's good external order elsewhere—well-painted doors and windows or patiently tended plants and flowers. When you realize the potential of your porch and decide to do something about it, however, don't make radical construction changes, or even build from scratch, without following procedural guidelines. As is the case with most alterations, you're best advised to seek a permit *before* going ahead. So grab your phone book and seek advice from the local planning department.

Adding a Porch

Not all houses have porches. Indeed, some homes that don't have porches are fine as they stand, architecturally speaking, and adding a porch would ruin an otherwise attractive façade. However, many houses would greatly benefit from the addition of a porch. The burning question, though, is what style would suit *your* house best? Don't panic! The good news is that your house itself should be able to answer this question for you. If your home has good architectural roots, they should be sufficiently inspiring to guide you. You won't be happy with the result if you add a Georgian porticoed entrance to your new-build cookie-cutter semi or affix an architectural symphony of concrete

Case Study: Forty-Year-Old Grannies

After

Problem: There really wasn't a before, as such! Sure, there was a back yard but it was overgrown, unloved, and neglected. What's more, getting to the back yard involved leaving the kitchen by a side door, walking around the house, and going on what seemed like a five-mile hike.

Solution: Our challenge was simple. We needed to establish a walkway from the kitchen (with full building code approval), add French doors, and create a brilliant alfresco dining and relaxing area that would become a positive asset to this quaint wee house. As this was a potentially dark area of the property, we planned to paint everything white to reflect as much light as possible and substantially brighten things up.

Before

Plus Points
* None, to speak of, aside from the fact that there was ample room outdoors to hatch our decking plan.

Minus Points
* Overgrown garden
* Small window that desperately needed conversion into a door

After

The pink kitchen that lies off the new patio so benefits from the extra circulation space created by adding the French doors. Taking out the wall area and adding the simple French doors

effectively blurs boundaries between outdoors and in.

Having such a cute spot to sip a cappuccino in the morning elevates this home to a whole new level. What's more, casual wiry furniture doesn't consume too much eye space.

We built the deck big enough to accommodate a couple of sun loungers for when the mercury starts to ascend. Getting acquainted with the great outdoors was a whole new ball game to this household.

Side rails provide not only safety but also a visual continuing of the wall lines from the glossy pink kitchen that lies beyond. This simple technique serves to reinforce the feeling of a room outdoors.

Before

and glass to your Victorian home, no matter how much your heart yearns for Georgian or ultra-modern. You can't rely on a porch to change the underlying character of your home, but if it's constructed in the same style, it will enhance your home no end. So be realistic and remember our motto: "Think twice—build once!"

Finding Inspiration in Your House

To design a porch that looks like it actually belongs on your house, consider its inherent stylistic clues. Plunder the detail of your home's architectural character—look at roof lines, window details, eaves, posts, and rails—and mirror these in your addition. Some detail work that you duplicate may be subtle enough that it won't be noticed much (ogee-edged trim at the top of a porch post, for example) but other details, such as pillar girth or size of supporting walls, will look out of place if they don't match or complement the existing structure.

To ensure your new porch fits in, you'll also need to consider the materials from which it will be constructed and the proportions of the addition.

Materials

Choosing matching materials or materials that are sympathetic to your home's existing architecture is fairly straightforward. While the occasional house might warrant an all-stone porch, most houses benefit from porches that are constructed almost entirely from wood. To confirm this, simply drive through your neighbourhood checking out porches. You'll see that many are of wood construction with perhaps a little brick detailing.

What's the best way to piece together these combinations? The trick is to duplicate—or complement—materials that have already been used to build and trim your house. If you can't get your hands on the real thing (antique brick, for example), do the next best thing and replicate it as closely as possible with reproduction materials or even synthetics. Some heritage homes will have special guidelines that set out acceptable materials for the job—if you have even the slightest doubt, call the planners to discuss everything in detail.

Proportion

Proportion is an exacting science yet at the same time it can be somewhat ethereal. It's a potentially problematic area that can cause all manner of visual trauma and, while some people might not be able to put their finger on what's actually "wrong" with your home, they'll certainly know that something isn't quite right if the scale of your porch has been ill-conceived. The problem could be the size or shape of supporting posts, rails, or trim. Or it could simply be that your doorway is out of scale with its canopy.

Think this sounds like loads of work? Just imagine how much extra work there'll be to get it right … if you first get it wrong by cutting corners!

The Finished Porch

Whether you're now the proud owner of a new porch or the slightly puzzled owner of an existing but unsatisfactory one, the following guidelines will keep you on track to having a welcoming home entrance.

Maintenance

Make porch maintenance an annual job but if you can, deal with the little jobs as they occur and before they grow into bigger problems.

✳ Regularly clear leaves from the eavestroughs that run above your porch to ensure they don't clog and cause subsequent wood-damaging overflow.

✳ Keep on top of paintwork both outside and inside your doorway structure. Regular sanding of flaking areas and touching up with paint as required will lead to longer porch life.

✳ To make footing as safe as possible, use textured paints or position mats on the floor of the porch.

Clear the Clutter

One of the worst things you can do with your potentially fabulous porch is to treat it as a storage area. Approaching a house and discovering the front stoop is used as a stop-off point between the kitchen garbage bin and the local dump is a real turnoff. If you have nowhere else to store refuse until pickup day, at least remember the environment—sort it into recycling boxes and ensure the right things go to the right department! Buy colour-coded crates that can be stashed neatly together and make sure they don't overflow! Better still, stash the trash discreetly out of sight at the rear of your house.

Just as you would do indoors, divide everything else into "off to the dump with you" and "off to the closest charity shop with you"— then deliver the goods to the proper place! Now it's time to relax.

Using Your Porch

The list of useful functions your porch can potentially undertake is almost endless. On TV, *and* in private commission, we've dressed many porches as comfy dining areas and we've attired others as secondary warm-weather living zones. If you install safety gates to enclose young kids, porches can also make fabulous playrooms as long as constant supervision is available— particularly if your porch is at the front of the house.

Even if a porch isn't big enough to serve a useful purpose, you should still dress it to create good first impressions. You've maintained or built it, so go on—add a little panache! Hanging baskets are a great way to pump up the style stakes, though remember these can dry out in as little as an hour on especially hot or windy days. Tubs, pots, and planters are easier to maintain and with regular care are less likely to become arid. Choose hardy plants with brightly coloured flowers to act as a decorating accent against neutrally painted siding, pillars, or walls.

Case Study:
Lights, Camera, Clutter

Problem: Had a hurricane blown in? Did a family of hobos live here? And what about all that crazy clutter? If this is an outdoors relaxation zone, we'd rather stay inside. *Blimey*—this front step needed help! But no job is too big for your favourite design superheroes.

Solution: Getting started was simple—call a dumpster company and order their biggest bin. Underneath all that chaos lurked a fantastic spot for soaking up a little Canadian weather. We simply needed to exorcise the bad-taste demons.

Before

Plus Points
* Sound porch structure
* Level floor
* Lovely views onto front garden

Minus Points
* Staggering outdoors clutter
* Mismatched furniture
* Elderly sun-shield wicker blinds falling apart at the seams

After

It's hard to believe that what essentially amounted to a good tidy-up—and a lick of paint —transformed this little porch from drab to fab! Add some casual seating, wooden blinds, and an indoor fireplace to make this a great space to chat with friends and relax at the end of busy days.

Our homeowner now has a completely rebranded space that positively oozes outdoor beach-house style. And, as a gentleman who loves to entertain his neighbours with cocktails on balmy evenings, he now has the perfect spot!

New wood window dressings provide open-and-shut protection—and a whole load of style into the bargain!—when Canadian breezes blow.

Comfy outdoor plastic wicker seating provides the perfect solution to running in and out when the weather isn't playing ball. This sofa can stay where it is all year round. Simply remove the cushions when the weather changes.

Comfy cushions, striped floor rugs, and a handy weatherproof table (from the same set as the sofa) provide a setting that positively screams settle down!

The drum-shaped indoors fireplace cuts a seriously stylish dash in crystal-clear heatproof glass. Gel-fired, it's easy to use and will help take the edge off cooler Canadian evenings.

Before

Case Study:
Bad Design: Guilty as Charged

Problem: Oh dear. This sunroom looked more like a garden shed! Looking the worse for wear, it was entirely unwelcoming in three seasons. And as far as winter sitting was concerned? Forget it! And, call us old-fashioned, but we think rooms should have furniture.

Solution: This was a massive challenge—knock down the entire garden room and rebuild from scratch. The completed room had to relate, in design terms, to the living room to which it would connect; it would become a secondary sitting area and play area for the family's two young children.

Before

Plus Points

* Sorry, none! Apart, that is, from the ground upon which the forlorn structure sat.

Minus Points

* Dreadful dated wood panelling
* Cold winds rattling through the space
* No furniture to speak of
* Dark ceiling glooming up the space

After

We're particularly proud of this transformation. We tackled this house during the depth of winter so you can imagine the fun we had! The completed structure boasts undeniable architectural presence, a brand-new solid lumber floor, pristine paintwork, and twenty percent more floor space than the previous room could manage. What's more, a higher ceiling magnifies the proportions even further.

We dressed the finished conservatory with leather and suede effect upholstery and provided visual warmth and sunlight filtration via window blinds made from woven natural fabric.

A vase full of real twigs, a touchy-feely floor rug, and a few scatter pillows were all the final dressing required to complete our great new look. Little wonder that our homeowners were blown away!

Before

Decks

DECKS AND CANADIAN SUMMERS GO HAND in hand! They're the modern interpretation of the old verandah—a place to sit while sipping an iced drink, to relax with friends and family, to just sit and stare. You'll never be sorry you added one or refurbished the old one.

Planning a Deck

We're regularly asked about the secret to creating perfect decks and, as far as we're concerned, it all starts with another C&J mantra: "To fail to plan is to plan to fail." Whatever your construction material and style of deck, it's imperative that you properly plan everything to satisfy building code, aesthetics, and lumber tolerance. But don't panic too much—planning consent doesn't necessarily require the services of an architect or a drafting professional, but when applying for a permit (see below), an accurately drawn sketch will generally suffice to keep bureaucracy happy. If you're not confident to undertake your own build we'd recommend seeking out a good contractor. And of course the more experienced your builder, the better the results will be.

Deck-to-House Relationship

The relationship between the deck and house is a basic but important issue, as so many factors have to be taken into consideration. The style of your home, for example, will have an impact on the deck's design but there's no reason you can't mix it up a little. A deck doesn't have to stay as true to the house's nature as a porch does. Access in and out of your house should be properly considered—your project will grow

arms and legs if you have to factor in the costs of a new door. Remember that a door that opens out will also limit the useful space on your deck.

And of course size is important! We avoid creating decks that are out of scale with the homes to which they're attached, and we try to work around existing horticulture wherever possible so as not to disturb nature. We've even been know to build decks around trees to avoid having to take down a beautiful specimen. Find a fault, make a feature, say we! Finally, bear in mind that if you have a sloping garden or yard, you'll need to invest in extra building materials to create a level surface.

Remember: Decks have a way of being too small once they're built—suddenly tables, chairs, and plant containers are jostling for space, so be realistic about the size of yours. Take your tape measure and check out friends' decks if you have trouble imagining how much space these items will take up.

Building Permits

It might surprise you to discover that most municipalities will require a building permit for the construction of a deck, especially if it's to be attached to your house or if the proposed height is more than 30 inches above ground. As always, it's better to work within legal guidelines as not doing so will inevitably come back to haunt you. Even home insurance can potentially be invalidated for accidents on what is technically (and we know this sounds dramatic) *illegal* terrain. So be warned! Doing it all by the book, however—and adhering to planning

Case Study: Clutter Nutter

Problem: Was our homeowner running a grocery store from this rough-and-ready mud room? And what was going on with all that clutter? And if Guinness World Records held a category for most out-of-proportion chandelier, surely this was a winner. Talk about making a poor first impression! But we had a plan.

Solution: Our challenge was colossal. Call time on the cereal boxes, banish the mess, and address storage issues into the bargain. And one last thing—it's a mud room, after all, so we needed to provide somewhere to sit and take off outdoor shoes before stepping into the house.

Before

Plus Points

* Good structural integrity
* Level floor surface
* Generous proportions so space could be reborn to create a great first impression

Minus Points

* Staggering clutter
* Jumbo light fitting was a real head-banging problem!
* Nowhere to leave coats and shoes

After

A warm sunny colour scheme enlivens the mud room and creates an instantly welcoming first impression. Surprising just how much can be achieved with a pot of latex, isn't it?

A slick wall of fitted wardrobes (not shown here) provides plenty of stash zones for coats and jackets and other items that need to be stored between showers and even seasons.

Secondary storage with a comfy padded top creates somewhere to both take off and store footwear!

The scaled-down overhead lighting (not shown here) is far more appropriate to a room of this size. That massive chandelier simply had to go!

Final dressing via window blinds, an attractive (and, importantly, machine-washable) floor rug, and decorative planting completes the lived-in look. As is so often the case, it's all in the final styling.

We connected the newly remodelled mud room to the living room beyond by specifying the same floor covering for both areas. It's a simple tried-and-tested method that builds relationships between zones.

Before

guidelines—can result in wonderfully useful walkouts or terraces that will add a whole new dimension to your home.

As we mentioned above, an accurate sketch will be needed when applying for the permit.

Materials for Deck Construction

Cedar, redwood, and pressure-treated pine are all sound choices for the surface of the deck. Each genus is famed for its resistance to moisture, rot, and decay, and although they each look different when new, they all tend to weather to a similar shade of grey over time. Whether you buy from Home Depot or a specialist timber supplier, make sure that you know what you're doing. Just for the record (and so you can enjoy the science bit!), the process of pressure-treating literally forces preservatives into the wood to protect it from termites and rot-inducing elements such as mould and fungus. (Teak is also great but it can be hugely expensive so it's best to leave that particular option to the boating industry!)

It's a sore point for us but, for a country so rich in timber, you Canadians often like to fake it (as you do in your basements with all that terrible "timber" cladding!) by using plastic boards or wood and plastic formulas. These products require special fastening systems and special installation techniques but your big-box store or installer will help with any questions you

may have. We concede that plastic has extra durability and protects little feet from splinters.

Maintaining the Deck

No matter your deck materials and design, whether a modern structure with myriad weird angles or a simple one-level patio area, it's crucial that you guard it from the elements. If you don't choose pressure-treated timber, it's almost a certainty that problems will occur.

However, pressure-treated wood requires maintenance to ensure it always performs as expected. True, it won't really rot if you don't maintain it, but it will still be subject to weather just like untreated timber and it can contort, shrink, and crack. With timber vulnerability at the root of our concern, here is our ultimate guide for lumber longevity.

✳ Use a power washer on pressure-treated wood at least once a year (preferably at the start of every season) to remove grit and grime. Doing this will also help reveal the original tones and patina of your flooring.

✳ Treat your timbers! At the start of each season, apply a top-notch wood preservative to inhibit moisture damage.

✳ Pressure-treated wood can (contrary to popular belief) be stained for protection against the rigours of everyday life. For best results, clean your wood (as before) with a power washer, then allow to dry. Apply a couple of coats of stain to suit your outdoor scheme.

Remember: With proper maintenance, a well-made deck constructed from pressure-treated wood can last twenty years or more.

Paint versus Stain

Some people like to colour their decks with specialist deck paint, but most choose to highlight the natural beauty of decking timber by applying a clear or lightly stained finish. If you do choose paint, it's really important to use a stain-blocking oil or alkyd primer first as protection against the elements. This done, apply your sheen and enjoy!

In general, the best finishes are those that soak into the wood, and not those that simply provide a surface film. A heavily pigmented "solid" stain isn't really recommended for decking because it shows wear pattern and tends to peel.

There are various important characteristics you should look out for in any of the options you consider. First, the finish should be waterproof (and not simply water-resistant), and second, it should offer UV protection to ensure your wood doesn't fade or bake in the heat. Third, if mildew is a potential problem, your finish should contain a mildew inhibitor. It doesn't cost anything to ask, so always spend time in conversation with the experts at your local building centre or garden store. And if staff can't answer your questions? Take your business elsewhere!

C&J'S
Top 10 Tips to Create a Perfect Deck or Porch

1 Develop a strong visual relationship between inside and outside.

2 Investigate building code and planning requirements before starting work.

3 Lighting is just as important outside as it is inside so employ the services of an electrician and wire everything correctly so you can enjoy the space to its best advantage.

4 Position small in-ground spotlights at the side of steps, and light back and front doors with sensors that flick to life as you approach.

5 Dress to impress—clever planting in pots and tubs is the simplest way to add style to outdoor space.

6 Opt for stains that penetrate the wooden surface of your deck or porch rather than those that simply sit on top of timber.

7 Practise good outdoor housekeeping! Debris that clogs grooves between deck boards will trap moisture, which may in turn encourage mildew and rot.

8 Be respectful of the existing style of your home as you plan this addition.

9 Scan your neighbourhood for porch inspiration and take photos of those you like. To help visualize the final effect, make a 3D model or plot everything out on graph paper.

10 And finally—give your outdoor space proper function. Clear the clutter and get ready to host that candle-light supper you've been promising your friends for ages!

Special

Requirements

Rooms to Grow

NEVER LET IT BE SAID THAT INTERIOR DESIGN IS AN EASY INDUSTRY! BUT creating children's rooms can be *particularly* tricky! You see, kids' rooms (never mind their occupants!) are a law unto themselves. Potentially self-contained—and therefore often private—worlds, they can be 24/7 hideaways in which your kids will sleep and breathe their way through their tiny lives!

Quite unlike adult rooms, these junior domains have an entirely different set of rules and regulations. Popular culture can *dramatically* influence their design, but decorating and designs should be tempered not only by what's cool for kids but by a whole host of other factors, such as growing older and sharing spaces with siblings. Our designs have at their very root a belief in the need for environments that are rewarding and fun. Add in living, eating, and sleeping, not to mention hide-and-seeking—and general shrieking—and it's clear that when designing kids' rooms, we—and you—have our work cut out.

Look Before You Leap

AS WITH ANY DESIGN, WE RECOMMEND *thorough* planning. Adaptability in these rooms is crucial so space can change as years advance (or as other children are added!). Ease of maintenance is similarly important. And of course kids' rooms have to be many things at one time:

* A safe private world into which kids can escape when they need to

* A safe play zone

* A space (if nowhere else is available) where homework can be undertaken

* A comfortable place to sleep

One of the fundamentals to a successful project is a clean, washable, and comfortable background that can be modified (with limited fuss and expense) as time passes and tastes fluctuate. Our watchword is forever *flexibility*. Kids' passions alter more frequently than adults' and the last thing you want to deal with is a complete tear-down six months after your child's allegiance springboards from Batman to Superman or from Barbie to My Little Pony.

C&J'S TIP

We have loads of nephews and nieces so we know that the younger contingent has some very set ideas about what they like and don't like. Children are more likely to care for their spaces if they've been involved in the design from the outset. So discuss expectations with your child and run through design possibilities before moving plans forward.

Where to Start

WE APPROACH KIDS' ROOMS A BIT differently from other rooms in a house. Although safety is a concern in all rooms, especially bathrooms and kitchens, it is paramount in kids' rooms and thus is our first concern.

Safety First

Before we look at the best way of pulling together all the requirements, we feel compelled to have a quick health and safety briefing! Children, particularly young ones, need to have safety taken care of for them so they can get on with the serious business of having fun. So, we'll get our safety check out of the way first before moving on to the fun bit!

C&J'S
Top 8 Safety-First Tips

1 Tiny fingers are easily trapped in door hinges, so fit plastic safety mechanisms. Pioneered years ago by one of the biggest fast-food chains, they are easy to install and make tremendous sense. You can find them in most home building stores.

2 Ensure all window cords, blind chains, and curtain pulleys are safely tucked out of harm's way. Sadly, each year, there are accidents and deaths where children have become trapped in the workings of seemingly innocent window apparatus. Similarly, ensure there are no trailing electrical cords and that all plugs are fitted with childproof fronts.

3 Windows should be fitted with childproof locks that allow for good ventilation yet limited opening.

4 We're cautious about bunk beds, although they are manufactured to strict safety guidelines. We are especially reticent to introduce them where children are under eight. That said, we've visited many homes where bunks have been installed without any problems but—we remain wary.

5 We never install open fires or gas fires in kids' rooms. We don't even need to explain why …

6 Similarly, if there are exposed radiators to contend with, we'd counsel keeping them on a separate thermostat so they don't become too hot. If this isn't possible, install a decorative safety screen in front to protect delicate fingers.

7 Scatter rugs laid on hard flooring should have anti-slip mats under them to protect against slipping or other accidents.

8 Never fit shelves at a low level. It might seem like the obvious thing to do, but if we had a dollar for every time we've heard about injuries when kids have careered headlong into the edges or corners of these shelves, we'd be very rich indeed!

Transitional Rooms

IF ROOMS HAVE BEEN DESIGNED IN TOO thematic a fashion, subsequent change will be more difficult. However, if rooms have been given a neutral backdrop, it will be much easier to effect change, so bear this in mind *ahead* of any project.

Ensure that play tables can later double as homework desks. Buy furniture that has loads of leg room to accommodate your offspring as their legs stretch! In essence, think ahead in the same way you might if buying clothes. Colour can easily be adapted and mood modified if different walls are used for accent. Temporary novelty decals and stickers can be removed and lighting can be made moodier if dimmer switches are added.

C&J'S TIP

At the outset, avoid novelty-shaped beds or wardrobes because elements such as these will make your child cringe as the passion for dinosaurs or Hello Kitty passes! Instead, opt for timeless pot lights, which work well for kids of any age. As children get older, repaint brightly coloured furniture in more adult neutral tones and hang cork boards around the room to display pop concert tickets or other youthful paraphernalia. Rooms should be flexible enough to change design direction (and age suitability) at the drop of a hat.

Shared Rooms

CHILDREN NEED THEIR OWN SPACE, HOWEVER small, to help them assert their personality so it's important to find ways of dividing rooms if they have more than one occupant. Colour can be a perfect way to divide areas. Shelved storage can separate two parts of a room, and it will also provide a useful function and an answer to privacy. In one of our most successful projects, we sectioned off two separate bed areas in a shared room by using floor-to-ceiling curtains, on curved tracks, which slide back to create individual wee nests as required. Trellis screens, too, can be hung on hooks between bed areas and these provide useful hanging space for artwork, knick-knacks, or mementoes. What's more, their temporary nature means they can be moved or taken away as you and your child see fit.

Case Study:
A Star in Stripes!

After

Problem: Answers on a postcard please: What, exactly, is going on here? *Aye*, your guess is as good as ours! Sure, it's great to recycle and use hand-me-down furniture, but when nothing matches and everything is way too junky to remain in service, there's a problem!

Solution: Create a TV room for a feisty twelve-year-old who wants a room that's entertaining even if the TV is switched off!

Before

Plus Points
* Spare room given good use as kid's TV lounge
* Wood floor in good condition

Minus Points
* Terrible cast-off sofas
* Positively possessed window treatment
* Does this look to you like a fun room for a twelve-year-old?

After

We got rid of the old sofa, replacing it with just two smart chairs whose leggy nature takes up less eye space than solid upholstered pieces, making proportions feel more generous. A few comfy cushions add a burst of colour and something to cuddle up to. Removable, machine-washable cushions make this kid-friendly, too.

We love to challenge the idea that small rooms can't handle big patterns, and that's why we decorated this tiny room with a bold stripe.

The existing wood floor was in good condition but didn't fit with our colourful vision. The simple solution was to add an area rug. For a low-cost design but a quality product, hit your local carpet warehouse, pick a colourful remnant, and have it whipped and bound.

We decided to chuck out the old fish tank and hang an ultra-modern landscape flat-screen fish fantasy instead! Remember, of course, that fish are living creatures and need to be cared for —they're not just pretty faces! And if there's nothing on the telly, you can just sit there and gaze at your little pals—very relaxing!

Overhead pendant lights can be quite harsh, unless your lamp shade is fitted with a diffuser. A diffuser can be fabric, frosted glass, or acrylic and acts like a screen to shield the bulb and produce a softer effect.

Kids' rooms should be fun and exciting, so when it comes to modern window dressing, you'll find that string's the thing! Rather than adding standard curtains, we decided to echo the vertical nature of the wallpaper by adding a string drape to create a fiercely funky window.

Before

Colour

A CAREFULLY SELECTED COLOUR PALETTE WILL stimulate senses—however, while soft shades such as pink and blue may be appropriate for the very young, we generally use more confident shades to inspire children's sense of drama, excitement, and fun. That said, too much bold colour can create an enclosed oppressive feel. By all means let children guide you, but ensure you don't create rooms that are gloomy and cold. Use paler backgrounds and then accent in more dramatic shades or use toys, artwork, and textiles as colourful accessories. Colour can also be added by using a growing range of wall stickers and transfers that are easily found in craft and DIY stores. Temporary colour is great news because children change their tastes almost overnight, so anything you can do to make their rooms more adaptable will make changes easier in the future.

Whichever paint colour you choose, be sure its finish is at least wipeable—or better *washable*—so you can remove crayon marks, pen scribbles, or the general rough and tumble of kids' playtime! And remember you have options (see our paint section on pages 280 to 285). Matte latex, for example, is less durable than satin finish so study manufacturers' specifications to find the most appropriate product for your job.

Magnetic Paint and Other Novelty Products

Magnetic paint (a harmless metal constituent that provides "grab") is a fun product that comes in a range of colours. However, if you can't find a colour you like, use a coat of standard latex over it. You can turn areas of your kids' rooms into magnetic play zones where lightweight fridge magnets, pictures, or letters of the alphabet can be stuck up and repositioned.

Fluorescent or glitter paints are great fun too, although their appeal can diminish as your child's fascination with stellar configurations is replaced by a fascination with stars of a more earthly nature. Novelty products, while great at the time, can suddenly lose their appeal.

Boys versus Girls

The traditional choice of pink for a girl and blue for a boy can, from our experience, be limiting—whether it's paint or furniture you're choosing. Should you wish to swap children from room to room at a later stage, you might just find a very disgruntled ten-year-old boy trying to make sense of a Barbie-pink paradise that makes him feel distinctly uncomfortable. We tend to make our schemes as gender *non*-specific as we possibly can, and we avoid thematic design wherever possible. Again, the secret lies in accessories as these can be easily changed as tastes shift. If you still want to add pattern, opt for stripes, spots, or simple blocks of colour that will provide restrained personality while still keeping your kids well and truly stimulated.

C&J'S TIP

Blackboard paints, while fun, are better applied onto panels of particle board or MDF (medium-density fibreboard) or specially designed portable boards (with dust-catching lips at the bottom) rather than directly onto walls. Erasing chalk creates great dusty clouds so it's better contained on a dedicated movable surface. Better still, get your kids into the habit of using a damp cloth to "rub out" and contain dust mountains even further.

Flooring

FLOORING IN CHILDREN'S ROOMS NEEDS TO BE tough enough to deal with the rough and tumble of junior life and should be neutral enough to move from one stage of childhood to the next without being rigidly anchored to the past. So forget the Little Mermaid carpet or the Batman equivalent! Heavily themed flooring is a definite no-no (here's where your negotiating skills might come in!), so always choose a product where design cues come from colour rather than pattern. This way you can tailor the environment as your child grows older.

Carpet

As the backbone to your scheme (however colourful it eventually becomes), choose a low-key hard-wearing carpet that is both washable and stain-repellent. Even the most fastidious kids will drop the occasional paint pot or knock over a food tray, so anything that allows you to deal with crises is great news. Bright shades will date so make colour statements with other less expensive elements of your design. Where we can, we use carpet tiles, so that damaged areas can be replaced should problems arise. Just remember to buy a few extra and store them away.

Bear in mind that tighter weaves and shorter piles will be easier to clean and will be kinder to those with allergies. Always check composition before purchase!

Cushioned Vinyl, Linoleum, or Manufactured Products

Manufactured flooring such as vinyl, linoleum, and faux wood and tile make great sense as they deal better than most other flooring with spills or accidents. Cushioned vinyl is soft underfoot and, if you select a wood effect finish or a plain shade, you can still add vibrant colour with washable rugs or mats. Don't forget to use anti-slip mats under rugs to protect against unwanted movement as you and your kids navigate play areas.

Wooden Flooring

If you're one of the lucky Canadian homeowners who still has the old 2- to 3-inch wood floorboards, you're on to a winner! These boards can be sanded and revarnished several times and painted or recoloured as tastes dictate. And the good news is that floor painting is a whole lot easier than you might imagine! With a growing range of specialist paints on the market (we recommend a brand called International, which is fantastically hard-wearing) it couldn't be easier.

C&J'S TIP

Before starting to work on floors, ensure they are free from protruding nails, screws, or splinters, all of which can cause injury if left unattended.

Case Study:
Boring Boys' Room!

Problem: Boring, boring, and boring—just how bland can a kids' room get? Perhaps excitement and stimulation come from elsewhere, as this room is the decor equivalent of a political broadcast.

Solution: We hoped to make this room grow up and transform into an exciting space of which any youngster would be proud.

Before

Plus Points

* A good attempt but rather bland
* Solid wood floor

Minus Points

* Posters scattered on a wall are little more than wall clutter!
* Room is boring. Zzz...

After

When using colour in a child's room, try to establish a balance between being too invigorating and being too boring. We painted a punchy orange and green squared target to add excitement but positioned it at the head of the bed so it's not in eye line when the child is trying to sleep.

When we were fanning through a catalogue of coloured wood flooring, we suddenly thought, "Why not use two colours rather than just one to create our very own striped pattern?" Doing this cost the same as choosing one colour and took the same amount of time to install, but it looks decidedly different!

Treat kids' rooms like adults' rooms and provide bedside tables, controllable lighting, and accessories. Taking an adult approach shows respect for your child and should ensure that they respect their surroundings too.

Show your child how to use storage from an early age and they may well continue using it. Provide plenty of drawers, wardrobe space, and shelving for your little one! And remember: kids mimic their parents, so if you're a bit of an untidy slob *chez vous*, your children might be similarly inclined.

Soften things up with fluffy floor rugs, bed throws, and squashy toys—we all love our rooms to be tactile and beautiful, but kids really appreciate the extra stimulation.

C&J'S TIP

Just as the fireplace is generally the focal point in the living room, so too is the bed the main visual aspect of most bedrooms. Choose an accent wall (where the bed will sit) and add colour here via paint or paper, and, of course, bedding.

Flexible Furniture

BEDROOM FURNITURE CAN BE PRETTY simple—a bed, a dresser, some storage units, and perhaps a bedside table are the basic requirements. But that doesn't mean deciding exactly what to buy is easy. Just about the worst thing you can do is invest in an expensive bedroom suite only to find that, a year down the line, your little prince or princess has grown tired of it. All of a sudden it's World War III and you're starting from scratch. Because kids' furniture is considered "niche market," it's often pricier than adult design so we always steer clear of car-shaped beds or fairytale-castle-shaped cots. We find it better to add personality through linens and duvet sets than be forever restricted by what was *previously* hot news for your children.

Search out flexible "intelligent" furniture that will grow with your child. An ideal choice is

C&J'S TIP

"Make do and mend" and a little lateral thinking will result in a collection of adaptable furniture that will serve a very useful purpose. Involve the kids by re-versioning items with their help. There's no reason that previously discarded junk furniture can't be brought to life with a lick of paint and a new set of knobs or handles. Check for lead content in paint on older pieces, even if you're painting over with lead-free paint. DIY stores sell check-up kits to set your mind at rest. Better safe than sorry!

modular storage that can be added to (or subtracted from) as required. Interconnecting box storage or rack systems will offer flexibility as your child moves through different periods of life. And anything that has wheels or casters will allow for the constant adaptation of space.

For maximum future-proofing, avoid miniature chairs and tables, which your young ones will soon find embarrassing (not to mention outgrow!) as they mature. Instead, opt for squashy beanbags or comfy seating cubes that will still have a worth as time goes by. Basket chests and trunks, too, can make for brilliant junior furnishing and the latter can be decorated and then repainted as years pass.

Choosing Children's Beds

As we explained earlier, adults spend approximately a third of their lives in bed but children spend even longer! Via earlier nights or a reluctance to detach from their duvets on a cold morning, your brood can be a sleepy bunch! With this in mind, it's crucial that you make the best buying choices to get the most from your children's formative years.

Children have almost limitless imagination, not to mention that innate ability to create something out of almost anything. Indeed how many times, as a child, did you make a den by pushing two chairs together and draping a blanket over the top? And how often did you transform the cupboard below the stairs into a

secret world from which adults were barred? The child's mind has an admirable ability to imagine a host of wonderful scenarios, from pirate ships to fairytale castles, from dragons and dungeons to race-car pit stops—thus our reluctance to select novelty beds for our projects. Imagination often provides far more … for far less! Let the kids create their own fantasy and you can stick to the provision of a safe and comfortable place to sleep and rest.

Bunk Beds

Bunk beds have long been popular with kids and parents alike due to their flexibility and the fact they're space savers when rooms are small yet need to accommodate more than one bed. Working on a "stack 'em high" principle, they

make good sense as long as safety is considered at all times. If bunk beds are anywhere near ceiling lights, or if children are within reach of cables or electrical cords, we'd recommend bringing in an electrician to move wiring to a safer position. Avoid positioning beds near window blinds or near any type of cord that could present a choking hazard.

One of the best features of bunk beds is their adaptability. Generally constructed from paintable wood or metal, they're available at pretty much every price and, when installed imaginatively, they can be great fun. The best types are those that can grow with your child. Search for models where the "ground floor" can be easily converted into a comfy seating area (when a second bed isn't required) or where the lower level can be reconfigured as a nifty study area for junior, as required.

If space is an issue, consider hiring a carpenter to build something that is exactly tailored to your space. You could also have custom storage incorporated as a further space saver.

Double-Duty Beds

With so many toys and other junior paraphernalia to be considered, we advise seeking out beds with hidden storage and drawers. It could even be that a traditional bed raised from the floor on legs will give you all the space required to stash linens and toys in trunks or wheeled trays that can be whizzed in and out as required.

Another type of double-duty bed is a baby crib that is so flexible it can be transformed into a young child's bed and then into an adult-sized bed as required simply by removing the side bars and installing full-length struts and a large mattress. There are many such "grow with your child" beds on the market and, with competition fierce, prices have dropped.

Futon

Often maligned (and for no good reason!) the good old-fashioned futon is a perfectly acceptable kids' bed as long as you invest in a good-quality product with a firm but comfy mattress. Space saving to the max (by day they fold into deep sofas to free up floor space and by night they fold back into funky, comfy beds to tempt your child's eight hours), they're traditionally low slung and have a trendy Oriental feel, which can be easily incorporated into a host of design looks, from brightly coloured Chinese to loft-look living with a twist.

Sofa Beds

Sofa beds are, like futons, foldable. They are either constructed on a tension-sprung base or built from dense foam. If you want to create a look that's more living room than bedroom, choosing a sofa bed is a practical solution and a stylish way to adapt space as your kids grow up.

Multi-Purpose and Double-Duty Rooms

LET'S BE HONEST—WHO COULDN'T USE MORE SPACE AT HOME? PROBLEM IS, though, that the only real way to achieve this dream is to either move or extend. Both these options can be potentially costly (not to mention problematic) but there is something you can do to use your available space more efficiently and more cost-effectively. The best way to make more out of less is to try multi-purposing.

The multi-purpose space or "double-duty" room can either be a blessing or a curse depending on how you approach the matter. Get it right and your home will be streamlined and efficient ... but get it wrong and you'll end up with a work zone that's more like a war zone!

Test Yourself

WE'RE THROWING A CHALLENGE AT YOU—how would you solve the following dilemmas?

Scenario 1: You have the smallest condo in Canada but still need to eat, sleep, play, and get up to a few more things besides ...

Scenario 2: You actually have a sizeable home but it needs to be extra flexible to cope with expanding needs ...

Time's up! Didn't get very far? Never mind—we can help! The good news is that you actually can squeeze many functions into one room. But the secret, of course, is learning how to pull it all off with style, grace, and harmony.

If your idea of multi-purpose means little more than plopping your PC on the kitchen table, you're definitely in the market for some much-needed C&J salvation.

How to Create Double Duty

ARMED WITH ANOTHER OF OUR FAVOURITE mantras—this time it's "Let your lifestyle dictate your homestyle"—the first thing you should do is make a list of all the things you need from each space. Next, start to examine how each need can be satisfied. Factor in all possible extra functions (things like home office, workout space, home cinema, sewing room, kids' play area) and think carefully about how your rooms can be carved up to accommodate each. While you're doing this, assess areas and functions no longer needed. Hopefully when you've done this, you'll see how your home can be made to feel much more efficient. If everything is still all as clear as mud, help is at hand. Here are our top tips for squeezing multiple functions into one standard-sized home.

Make More of Your Least-Used Rooms

Decide the best place for multi-tasking. Do you have a formal room that's rarely used or does your dining room cry out for dinner parties while you and the family prefer chowing down in the kitchen? Go on—make your least-used room the perfect spot to do *several* new things ... at once! Occasional-use dining rooms are perfect double-duty spaces—pop in an office (discreetly tucked into a lovely armoire) and instantly—two functions in perfect harmony. Add some wall-to-wall bookcases and suddenly you have a library! With eat-in potential ...

In Teddy's tiny, narrow bedroom there wasn't space for bedside tables so we designed a headboard with additional storage for accessories and other items tucked at the rear.

Use Every Corner

What's with that strange wedge-shaped space under the stairs, eh? Could it be a little office? Or how about that extra-wide hallway that simply screams potential? If you made that into your dining area, could you make your dining room into a much-needed family room?

Think about customizing awkward nooks and crannies with shelving, for instance, to create valuable storage space (ideal for housing kids' toys or a sewing kit, perhaps?) or adding a table-height surface with a folding chair hidden below as the ideal homework zone for kids.

Perhaps your dream model railway village could be set up in a shallow box stored under your bed. Pop on some casters and you've created roll-out, roll-in entertainment! It's all about analyzing your available space and making the very best of what you have.

Zone Out

With multi-function spaces, the most important thing to do is to keep each function clearly defined. Try using furniture (tall, open shelving stacks, for instance) to delineate space and, if you can, create zones within zones—a media unit and sectional sofa will clearly mark out your TV area, while a dining table and chairs will announce where food is served. Treat each as a separate "vignette" by using area rugs to clearly map out where one function starts and another one begins. You could also build in visual barriers to zone out space—a low-slung sideboard with a lamp either side looks great as a "fence" between zones or try decorative screens, fabric panels, tall house plants, or even sculptures on plinths as visual partitions.

One for All and All for One

Identify a single vision for your entire room with regard to style, colour, and period, and then piece in various functions around this scheme. Treating a multi-task room with a single design identity creates harmony so use complementary colours throughout and furnish using similar styles. A dining table and a coffee table, for example (even though they might be positioned in completely different sections of a room), would immediately "connect" if constructed from matching wood. Or perhaps an accent wall tone in the study area is all you require to perfectly "bond" with another shot of the same tone, only this time executed as upholstery detail in the living area or perhaps table dressing in the dining zone.

C&J'S TIP

Don't think of your house as a series of rooms ... think of it as a series of interconnecting zones, each of which has a relationship to others.

Be Flexible

Use "intelligent furniture"—by which we mean furniture that has a multi-function nature, such as a sofa that folds flat to become a bed, a coffee table that can be raised to become a dining table, or an upholstered ottoman with removable top that's the perfect seat, toy box, or foot stool. If you have to locate an office in the bedroom, rather than simply sticking a desk at the foot of your bed, make part of your closet a dedicated work station. Hire a carpenter to build you a camouflaged pull-down shelf that will neatly drop, as required, to create the perfect work spot or sewing corner.

When buying furniture, consider all the ways it can be arranged. Flexibility is paramount. A modular sectional sofa, for instance, can be moved around to accommodate different functions—seating for six or lie-back lounging for four. Factor in these choices before purchasing and—here we go again!—"Think twice, buy once."

Make a Wheel Difference

For real flexibility, consider portable items that can be moved around as required. Think of a couple of wheeled storage-cube tables. Now position one on either side of your sofa with a lamp on each and admire how elegant they look. Fancy a change? Simply remove the lamps, wheel the cubes into the centre of your space, and abracadabra—you've created the perfect coffee table. But there's more! Remove the lids and you have immediate access to all of your kids' toys.

Small-Scale Thinking

Don't overstuff rooms with too much furniture or too many functions—fewer, smaller items will leave more breathing space and rooms will appear cleaner and more efficient. To maximize space, for example, lose that "big box" PC in favour of a small, slim laptop that can be stored

away with ease. Or swap your elaborate outsize squashy chesterfield for a smaller compact sofa and a couple of chairs. Make a habit of searching out furniture that can be folded away and stored when not in use.

Design for Life

If you like the idea of positioning an office or work space in your kitchen, especially if you're starting from scratch, ask your planner to build for the future. In simple terms, this means incorporating a small office function into your layout so you're not left searching for somewhere to operate your business in a year or two. It could be as simple a job as positioning a narrow section of worktop on chunky legs and fastening it to one wall. *Et voilà*—you've got a breakfast bar … or somewhere to position your laptop and work at home. You choose!

Behind Closed Doors

If you can, try to locate added functionality behind closed doors. That way you can hide things when each task is complete. Here's an example of what we mean: We fitted a kitchen for a client whose entire condo measured just 335 square feet. We created a glorious white galley but, because our client works from home, we assigned one side to food-prep and the other to his freelance stock market business. To the naked eye, the long white room looks like a perfect (if rather minimalist) food prep heaven but what we created is actually a classic dual-function triumph. Open the doors on one side (hinged upward so as not to get in the way) and computer, files, fax, and photocopier are all suddenly revealed. One particular section of worktop pulls out to 18 inches to create a compact desktop where our chap can sit while studiously working on his clients' portfolios! Close the doors, push back the counter, and serene white culinary calm is restored.

Find a Fault—Make a Feature

If you have to store hundreds of fabric samples for sewing, art supplies for painting, or balls of yarn for knitting, try to keep everything in smart boxes arranged in a regimented manner. That way, housing a secondary function in any room will be efficient and pleasing to the eye. You'll be able to banish that huge pile of clutter lying to one side of your couch!

Discover that You're Big Downstairs!

Don't ignore one of your biggest assets. Instead, dive into the great Canadian basement to create new possibilities *chez vous*. Consider the benefits of a finished basement. Rather than having what's effectively little more than a dank messy storage zone, we're thinking guest suite, home office, cinema, children's play room, spa bathroom…. The choice is—and the added flexibility will be—yours!

Use Technology

If you have wi-fi internet, there's no need to wire each room individually or trail cables from zone to zone. Wireless technology offers optimum flexibility in your mobile office. Systems such as these take up much less space than multiple modems.

Double-Duty Artwork

Another of our clients who works from home is in the music business. Due to the plotting and planning that's required as part of her job, she needs whiteboards hung all round her space. If these were permanent, she'd find it hard to switch off at the end of the day. We designed the whiteboards so they can be turned over to reveal artwork that we carefully matched to the rest of her room. Thanks to thinking out of the box, she can literally put work behind her whenever she chooses!

C&J'S

Top 10 Items for a Double-Duty Shopping List

1 **Storage Ottoman:** seating, storage, and table all in one.

2 **Drop-Down Coffee / Rise-Up Dining Table:** double the function from one piece.

3 **Kitchen Storage Bench:** cookbooks and baking trays housed casually within seating at the kitchen table.

4 **Storage and More Storage:** simplify rooms by keeping everything boxed and hidden.

5 **Sofa Bed/Murphy Bed:** a guest suite in minutes and no extra room required.

6 **Coffee Table with Stashable Stools:** additional seating for four when you need it most.

7 **Extendable Dining Tables:** office or other work space as required.

8 **End Tables with Drawers or Shelves:** a stylish way to introduce extra surfaces and extra storage.

9 **Armoire:** use as home office, multimedia centre, or clothes storage. Particularly good for bedroom offices—and don't forget to pin storage sleeves to the inside of the doors to stash things like flat document files.

10 **Stackable Chairs:** fabulous sculptural chairs that look just as wonderful when stacked are easy to find these days!

Small Spaces, Large Spaces

NO ONE EVER THINKS THEY HAVE ENOUGH SPACE, NO MATTER THE dimensions of their house. It doesn't matter if your home is small or large, what really matters is that you use every inch for a purpose and that no space remains unconsidered. You might think you have a difficult house if it's small or is an open-concept condo, but if that small house has a spare room or your condo has obvious gaps between areas, you could be on to a serious winner. Large houses have their own challenges. These houses can seem unwelcoming or sterile because their owners haven't figured out what to do with all that space.

Fear not—we've got a great grab bag of helpful tips and advice for your situation, whether you've got too little space or too much.

Small Spaces

"A PLACE FOR EVERYTHING AND EVERYTHING in its place"—so goes the old maxim. It may be old but it's still one of our *truest and most used* home mantras. Good storage makes for great rooms. Period. So, with this in mind, go large on storage and low on clutter, especially when you're living in a compact space.

Try to incorporate storage in every room. Installing bookcases, shelves, and cabinets from floor to ceiling will give you loads of useable stash zones without eating up too much floor space. If you can, use wall-mounted shelves instead of floor-standing sideboards to further enhance the space.

Top 9 Ways to Increase the Feeling of Space

1 **Keep Walkways Defined.** When you can see floors, rooms look larger and you can easily move through the space. Keep taller, bulkier items on the walls and go low with sofas, coffee tables, and other furniture to keep eye lines clear. Don't push everything into corners and leave the centre clear—this won't make space look larger, it'll just make it look bare!

2 **Use Light Colours.** Dark colours can "draw in" a room and make it feel small, whereas lighter shades will open up space. You don't have to paint your entire home white—instead try pastels, neutrals, or naturals, all of which enjoy the same expansive qualities of white, while being much warmer.

3 **Blend Your Features.** Simplify your space by painting walls, trim, and detailing in slightly different shades of the same colour. Paring down in this way softens impact and helps a space look much larger.

4 **Reflect on Your Space.** Mirrors in any form are great for bouncing light and opening up space. We've clad entire walls with mirror, hung clusters of junk-shop mirrors across chimney enclosures, and used mirrored consoles and tables to enlarge perceived space. Glass tables and accessories can increase the feeling of space.

5 **Big Is Best.** Use a few well-chosen larger items of furniture instead of clusters of smaller items and avoid too many collectibles and knick-knacks in favour of one or two larger statement pieces.

6 **Pare Down Your Windows.** A simple blind or sheer fabric drapes will help keep windows defined and allow the maximum amount of light to pass through. Larger drapes consume too much wall space and absorb lots of light.

7 **Demand Double Duty.** Select furniture items that have a hidden extra function, such as a headboard with storage behind. Check out our multi-purpose chapter for more info.

8 **Maximize Light.** Electric light can be a very effective means by which to "increase" space. Use lighting to highlight each of the four corners of your room to expand its size, illuminate a row of art in a hallway with picture lamps to elongate perceived length, and brighten up dark nooks with spotlights to create a more expansive feel.

9 **Lose the Rubbish.** Declutter, declutter, declutter. Enough said!

Dealing with Large Spaces

IF YOU'RE FORTUNATE ENOUGH TO HAVE TOO MUCH space, then lucky you! But of course big isn't always best; indeed, large scale can also cause problems. Poorly arranged rooms may look bare or you might find it difficult to create good definition between functions. But worry not—we have some clever tricks up our sleeves …

C&J'S
Top 8 Tips to Use Large Spaces

1 Go Large. Scale up sofas and artwork and other accessories to fit the space—a small loveseat will look lonely in a large room so opt instead for a pair of huge sofas or an outsize sectional. Splash out on a giant coffee table and huge decorative floor lamps and bounce around on a king-size bed ...

2 Divide and Conquer. Use room dividers, smart double-sided display cabinets, or screens to break up space. Modern loft-style rooms can look great with floor-to-ceiling frosted glass panels, while open-sided bookshelves can serve two spaces at the same time.

3 Apply Colour Cohesion. Use the same colour palette in different areas of your room—your living zone, for example, could have a blue striped sofa, while the same blue could look good as napkin detail on the dining table at the other end of the same room.

4 Be Defined. With large rooms, the most important thing to do is to keep each function clearly defined. Try using furniture to delineate space and, if you can, create zones within zones—a media unit and sectional sofa will clearly mark out your TV area, while a dining table and chairs will announce where food is served.

5 Use Rugs to Define Space. Treat each function as a separate vignette by using area rugs to clearly map out where one function starts and another one ends.

6 Install Sliding Doors. Sliding doors or a modern concertina wall system will give you the flexibility of having one large room ... or two smaller spaces.

7 Create Interest Zones. Setting a console table with a huge flower arrangement gives a traditional look. You can also install three sculptures on plinths in a row for a minimalist, art gallery style at home.

8 Use the Space Differently. In a large bedroom there's no need to push the bed against the wall—pop it on a jaunty angle or bring it into the centre of the room.

Tight Budgets

IT DOESN'T MATTER WHAT YOU'RE RENOVATING—EVERYONE HAS A BUDGET. AND although yours might be lower than you'd prefer, it doesn't mean your dream home can't become a reality. We speak from experience. We've learned the tricks.

When we moved into our first apartment—a £26,000 tiny fixer-upper in Glasgow— we remodelled the hideous kitchen by changing counter tops and rejigging the existing units. Our new fridge cost just £5 as we bought it from builders who were ripping out a nearby restaurant. The entire reno cost just a few hundred pounds— and of course it looked fabulous.... Two years later we sold the apartment for £50,000. That's how we began the ascent up our own property ladder.

So we can say with some confidence: Stick with us and we'll show you how to get designer looks without breaking the bank.

Where to Start

THE FIRST STEP IS TO RENOVATE YOUR thinking and your attitude. Designing and creating a wonderful home should be a joyous undertaking (regardless of budget) so you should know that even a small budget can make a big difference. Good style isn't about being cheap and cutting corners, it's about planning realistic requirements and matching all of these with your available dollars.

Now that budget restrictions aren't going to stand in your way, you can take the next step. Look at the chosen room and ask what you want it to achieve and how you want it to look. Create mood boards or tear sheets (assembled from magazines and other printed material). Tie down all your ideas on paper—doing this, after all, costs nothing. Problem solving at this stage is really sensible and means you can address anything that's not right—do you have enough storage, is the room too dark, will there be enough seating? This analysis lets you move forward to the next step …

Look at the elements you already have. Does that old wooden floor just need a little sanding or refinishing to bring it back to life? Could your old sideboard be reborn with a change of colour and some new handles? Remember that a lick of paint can change the identity of any piece so let your imagination run wild.

Time to Purge?

Finally, try to be ruthless with what's staying and what's going. It just doesn't make sense to bring a gorgeous new sofa back to the ranch only to position it on that tatty, dog-haired old carpet. Replacing the carpet might throw your budget out of whack, but it could well be that it's money well spent … and speaking of money …

A simple change of colour—and some clever "visible spending" on a new marble top—has made a huge and very stylish difference to a dark and dated dresser.

Work Out Your Budget

AT THE BACK OF EVERY FANTASY HOME RENO there's a "paying for it" reality so it's crucial to be realistic about how much you have to spend *before* you start your transformation. Working out a budget for a reno isn't that different from working out a household budget—in fact, it is tied to your household budget. Scrutinize your monthly income and outgoings and include any money you may have ferreted away to help with the costs of the proposed reno. Being realistic about how much you have to spend will protect against subsequently living with the remorse of buying inappropriate (if less expensive) products. You don't want your new purchase to scream "costly regret" every time you walk into the room, do you?

Here's our simple rule: If you can't afford it, don't do it. But even if you're cash-strapped, don't completely give up. Do something that will still give you at least part of the look you hope to achieve! Imagine, for example, that you want to hang white wooden shutters to create a dreamy Cape Cod look, but their price is prohibitive. Are there options other than giving up? Almost always there are. In this case, are there less expensive window treatments that could provide that elusive Cape flavour? Would simple white wooden venetian blinds create a similar look?

New for Old

MORE MONEY GENERALLY GIVES YOU THE potential to buy more lovely things. If your budget is a bit short of your desired goal, you can add to your funds by selling off all the old stuff you no longer need. Online auctions, small ads in the local paper, or good old-fashioned yard sales can free your home from clutter while building up design funds. And don't just expect to raise nickels and dimes—there are big bucks to be made in castoffs.

When we remodelled our Toronto kitchen, our inner canny Scot came out. We sold the previous cabinetry and appliances via craig'slist. Employing a true entrepreneurial spirit, we cleaned them, then we dressed them, then we photographed them. Next we worked out the original cost of all the appliances and cabinetry *before* laying out our online advertisement describing the "bargain" kitchen in exacting detail. Our other option would have been to rip out a kitchen we didn't want and pay for a dumpster to take it away. *Hmm* … doesn't sound very Colin and Justin, does it? So we sold the old kitchen in its entirety for $5,000, with the bonus that our buyer had to remove the whole lot!

Get Your Shopping in Order

FIRST PRICE YOUR "PRACTICALS"—THINGS like rewiring and wallpaper hanging. This exercise will ensure that when your gorgeous $2,000 dishwasher is delivered, you know you've got the funds to have it plumbed in. Do some comparison shopping—hit the stores, browse catalogues, and scan the internet to research just how much your new pieces will cost and how much prices will vary. It's smart to prioritize your spending, so start off with room finishes—walls and flooring—then move onto larger items (like sofas and beds). The rest goes for accessories! By being organized in this way, you're less likely to indulge in a $400 vase when you've only got $1,000 to furnish your entire room … that's the way you end up sitting on milk crates!

Splash Out on Visible Spending

WHEN YOU'RE WORKING WITH A LIMITED BUDGET, YOU want to get the most out of your dollars. You want to be able to see what all that money went on! Splashing out on large statement pieces that will become the backbone of your room is a worthwhile outlay. These are items that will last, such as new flooring, custom cabinetry, or classically styled furniture—they are all significant enough to be noticed and all significant enough to give your room a wow factor. But you'll need to shop *carefully*. We'll use the wardrobe comparison again as an example. Imagine a perfectly cut Armani jacket teamed with a black skirt from Value Village. The Armani jacket should be "significant" enough to add luxury to the entire—even that VV skirt! Apply the same principles to your home—choose the element that's going to be your statement and build around it.

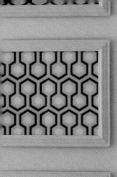
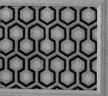

Other Considerations

HERE ARE SOME OTHER TIPS TO KEEP IN MIND WHILE YOU'RE DEALING WITH money matters.

* Set aside a contingency fund—ten to fifteen percent of your planned budget should take care of any unexpected expenses.

* Avoid impulse buys—stay "on message" when you're visiting favourite stores. And keep an eye on additional costs like local taxes or delivery charges.

* Factor in costs for tools and equipment—painting a room is a low-cost way to make radical changes, but don't forget to add in the cost of brushes, rollers, trays, ladders, and even dust sheets.

And Remember, Room Wasn't Built in a Day ...

IF YOU'D PREFER TO AVOID THE COST OF TACKLING A PROJECT IN ITS entirety, break the bigger job into smaller parts. Address individual aspects of the plan as and when you can. It often makes sense not to rush into large schemes. Instead, get a proper feel for what it is you hope to achieve. Then you can start transforming your space bit by bit. Ask any designer and they'll probably confess that they, too, have lived with rubble and ruin as they've embarked upon the transformations, layer by layer, of their own homes.

And, talking of designers, it could be that a great way to save money is actually to hire one! A good designer has all kinds of tricks and connections that will help you stretch your budget and should have the experience to save you a fortune by choosing the best colours first time round. Even if you don't want to commit to hiring a designer, there are still some great opportunities to be had. Don't be afraid to ask for free advice from furniture retailers or from the chaps at your local paint supplier. They are, after all, the experts and are paid to steer you on the right path. And make sure you pick up all those handy-hints leaflets from big-box stores—they might just have the answer you're looking for!

C&J'S
Top 10 Ways to Do More ... for Less

1 **Paint.** Painting a room is relatively inexpensive and will elicit maximum results for minimum effort. Good preparation costs nothing, but be sure to do it all properly and the finished results will deliver. If you're slapdash? Your results will be forever disappointing.

2 **Do It Yourself, But Do It Properly.** Do what you can, but don't be a "have-a-go hero" if you're simply not up to the job. Think how much you'd save if you could actually paint, tile, or make curtains ... and then estimate how much wasted time and cash there'd be if your home became a series of botched jobs. If DIY's not your thing, then try DFY—Done For You. Call in the pros!

3 **Use What You've Got.** Raid the basement, fish out Granny's old dresser, and give it a facelift. A lick of paint and some new handles could haul it out of the dark ages and make it worthy of becoming centre stage once again. Or reach for the sewing machine and make some new slipcovers for your dated sofa. Or drill holes and add some shelves to an old armoire to turn it into a media centre to house your TV or DVD player. Always think out of the box and look at things differently.

4 **Move Things Around.** Sometimes a good clear-up and a change of orientation is all that's needed to freshen your surroundings and provide a whole new look. So, with this in mind, move your sofa to the other side of the room, try your bed on another wall, or simply clear clutter and rearrange accessories to re-dress your space.

5 **Swap Skills.** Okay, so you're handy with a sewing machine but know nothing about electrics. So what are you going to do about your terrible kitchen lighting? Hold on a minute ... Your next-door neighbour's a friendly electrician, but he has terrible curtains. Why not offer to make some fabulous new window drapes in exchange for him fitting some overhead lighting? Think about swapping skills with friends, family, and neighbours as a way of "paying" for home improvements. Or get the gang round for a painting party in return for music, pizza, and beer!

6 **Search Out the "Scratch and Dent."** Ask around larger furniture stores to discover whether they offer discounts on "scratch and dent" damaged items, customer returns, or even last season's stock. Some department stores have dedicated clearance centres so it's well worth scouting around. We regularly buy *Home Heist* sofas from The Bay's clearance centre and they're always *fabulous!* Remember another of our mottos: "It's not *how much* money you spend but *how you spend* it that makes all the difference."

7 **Buy Off-the-Shelf Items.** Custom items generally cost a little more so try to stick to stock products whenever you can, even if that means adapting readily available stuff as required. Buy off-the-shelf picture frames but use matting paper to cut openings to fit your pictures. Jazz up store-bought curtains by sewing in linings to provide extra weight, or sew buttons, trims, or beading on to plain cushions and throws to add a low-cost, personal touch.

8 **Use the Internet.** Swap, sell, or search! Whatever you do, get on to the World Wide Web and sniff out those bargains! Not only is there a world of opportunity at your fingertips, but you'll also save money by avoiding the gas costs associated with driving around trying to find what you're after! Bear in mind, however, that there may be postage or delivery costs when you total up your bill.

9 **Try Seasonal Adjustments.** Design your room with a neutral backdrop and choose plain walls and furniture. Next, adjust your overall look by using cleverly selected accessories. Bear in mind that it's cheaper to change "decorative jewellery" than a whole room so, if you're a habitual decorator and constantly redesigning, let the seasons guide you.

10 **Shop Second-hand Stores.** Second hand doesn't have to mean second best so cast your decor net over charity stores, newspaper notices, online auctions, estate sales, and salvage yards for some fabulous home bargains. But just because something *appears* to be a bargain, it doesn't mean you should have it. Avoid "snatch and grab" impulse buys and invest instead in classic pieces that are solid enough to stand the test of time. Or buy items that can be transformed into useful pieces. We've reupholstered many an old sofa on *Home Heist* to give our homeowners their favourite couch back—but dramatically restyled!

Themed Rooms

WARNING! THEMED ROOMS ARE AN AREA OF GRAVE C&J CONCERN! AFTER ALL, who really wants to live in a Walt Disney–inspired living space with fibreboard castellation instead of crown moulding, car seats instead of sofas, and sand on the floor in place of carpet? Okay, so you adore everything medieval, you love rally driving, or you want to be forever reminded of that last holiday in Thailand ... But is literal theming really the answer?

The problem with themed rooms is that their creators tend to overplay ideas, ideas that—had they been better executed—might have made a good schematic starting point. It's all very well to be inspired by Thailand and to add Asian influences in a whispered way (sand-coloured walls, for example, rather than real sand on the floor) or to add a few medieval tapestry cushions rather than turning your space into a fortress because you happen to love the legend of Robin Hood. Similarly, if you're a car buff, a couple of racing green pillows or an artistically framed Le Mans print might be ample seasoning to remind you of the track rather than a coffee table made from car gear shafts or a pair of curtains made of starter flag. That type of design is a recipe for disaster.

The only area where we feel a little less worried about themed design is in children's spaces. These rooms are little worlds unto themselves. A fairytale palace for your little princess, or a *Pirates of the Caribbean* themed bedroom for your young sailor is okay, but we'd counsel a little caution when spending money on boat-shaped beds or castle-shaped chests of drawers. From our experience, children's tastes fluctuate frequently, and with this fluctuation can come the need for further financial investment.

Protecting Against Thematic Dilemmas

ONCE YOU SET OFF DOWN THE ROAD OF THE THEMED room or house, it can be hard to stop or turn back. Before you know it, you're overwhelmed with fake jungle, suits of armour, pioneer implements—or elements of whatever theme is leading you astray. Here's some solid advice to get you back on the straight and narrow.

Furniture Selection

Whichever look you follow, selecting your furniture carefully will avoid costly mistakes. Opt for classic pieces that can be reused as required. Working these standard pieces into your design will mean that, as the thematic novelty wears off, you can reuse these (hopefully more neutral) pieces as a starting point for your latest obsession. Our decorating mantra "Less is more" was never more relevant than here due to the fact that most themers simply can't stop and are tempted to purchase every item they see that corresponds with a favoured mood. Resist this temptation and limit yourself to high-quality pieces and to those that properly coordinate with other items in your space. Reject this guidance and your home will end up looking like a souvenir shop at the local theme park!

Hold Back!

To the best of your abilities, stay within your chosen colour scheme and use only coordinating and complementary colours, otherwise your scheme will begin to jar. Carefully consider every item and remember that just because something technically "fits" with the theme, it doesn't automatically mean it will fit with your space.

Creating a themed room does not mean anything goes! Your project, upon completion, should still be cohesive and comfortable. If you think you've gone overboard, you probably have. So take a few things back.

And, while you're at it, apply a simple rule of moderation to gifts given by well-meaning friends and relatives who can't help buying you new additions—another ceramic cow or Queen Mother memorial mug. It's guaranteed they'll pick up a trinket here or a gizmo there. However, there comes a time when you have to let them know you don't have space for any more gifts.

When you come across new items (even though you thought your look was complete), you gotta be tough! Either say no, or edit by taking something out before putting something new in. Perhaps you have similarly crazy friends who also love a Moulin Rouge–themed decor so do yourself a favour and give them that sexy fringed lamp (you know, the one with the lace stocking base).

C&J'S
Top 3 Suggestions for Using Themes

We're not saying you can't have a theme—we're just saying, first, you have to use restraint, and second, you need to respect the fundamental style of your house. The function or overall look of your room can also help determine theme. Here are some ideas to illustrate what we mean:

1 If you want your room to be a casual place in which to relax, perhaps a cruise ship theme could be good. However, before you go crazy with funnel-shaped coffee tables and ship-type clocks, exercise the less-is-more approach and you might just get away with it! Instead of being too literal, try being inspired by the beauty of teak deck finishes or classic art deco lines. A couple of Odeon sofas could be all you need.

2 If you fancy re-creating the elegant feel of a gorgeous country house in your dining room, don't slavishly try to re-create Buckingham Palace in miniature or it'll look, quite frankly, silly! Instead, opt for a few carefully selected antique pieces such as bergère chairs and add an over-mantel and a few period accessories to seal the deal.

3 If you're transforming an unused room into a den or home office, an affection for global travel could be a good starting point for a restrained theme. Opt for dark rattans and add touches of leather and perhaps an antique globe. But please—for the love of all that is right and just—steer clear of desks made from old travel chests, framed passports as artworks, and half a dozen clocks set to different world times!

In More

Detail

Using Colour

COLOUR IS AN EXCEEDINGLY COMPLEX TOPIC—INDEED, whole books have been written on each single colour! We could present an in-depth analysis about how certain colours are created and how each reacts to the naked eye. What's more, we could attempt to explain why some scientists believe that colour "memory" is passed down through DNA! Some commentators actually believe we are drawn to particular shades via "predisposed colour inheritance." They think that, because your grandmother loved blue, you're genetically programmed to feel the same way. One word from us: *Whatever!*

But come on—doesn't all that sound just a wee bit professorial and actually a tad boring? As a more realistic means of colour counsel, we'd much rather look at simple (but nonetheless important) breakdowns of what colour can do for your home and how you can use it to get the very best from your environments.

Although we *won't* be adhering to the "Your grandpa wore beige overalls so that's why you love taupe" theory, we do and *will* recognize that colour not only feeds and inspires the eye but also has physiological and psychological benefits.

Effect of Colour

COLOURS CAN AFFECT MOOD AND BEHAVIOUR, WITH SOME SHADES HELPING CONCENTRATION (soft greens and pale yellows, for example) and certain colours (such as vivid yellow) causing abject distraction. It's also worth noting that some colours are cold (deep blues, for example, can be particularly austere unless softened by the introduction of warmer tones), some warm (berry shades through to cozy autumnal tones), others calming (moss green and pastel shades generally), and some, lime green for example, are just way too energetic for certain rooms, such as bedrooms. It's always advisable to base colour choices not only on design and aesthetic but also on the temperature and mood of the environment. Try also to choose shades that will be tranquil and relaxing by night and refreshing by day.

The following section provides a nutshell description of what each of the most popular colors conveys—psychologically—and how each hue can benefit your home, whether on the walls, on the floor, or in accessories.

White

UNLESS YOU ADORE STARK MINIMALISM, AN all-white scheme can be rather austere. Used to "pop" other colours, however, it will provide decorating balance and visually "open" space. If you're hell-bent on a snowy scheme, pick softer white (or palest cream) tones to avoid glare.

Blue

CONTRARY TO POPULAR BELIEF, BLUE IS *NOT* just for boys. It's now considered a colour that appeals to both sexes in equal measure. Okay, when a child's still a baby or toddler, a little gender-specific scheming can often appeal, but as girls mature, their fondness for pink is often balanced by a yearning for blue.

Depending on the intensity of shade, blue can soothe and relax, making you feel more spiritual and centred. Which is great news if you fancy experimenting with this palette in the bedroom. What's more, it's reported to have educational benefits! So if you want to help your kids sail though their homework, opt for blue as it has been shown to improve concentration and therefore output!

Blue is also perceived as a refreshing and invigorating tone, making it a particularly relevant choice for bathrooms and laundry areas.

Red

RED IS CONSIDERED BY MANY TO HAVE THE opposite effect to blue and has even been shown to increase blood pressure! *And* it allegedly stimulates appetite, which goes part of the way to explaining why red (in its variant guises) was often chosen by Victorian decorators for their dining room projects. It's also considered a great conversation prompter so is regularly used in period British drawing rooms. And of course we know what we're talking about, because as you might just have noticed— we're British!

However, red is a very powerful colour so we'd advise limiting its use to accent walls and decorating "punctuation"—pillows, throws, and bedding, for example. If you overuse red, you'll look as if you're on red alert—proclaiming a state of high danger!

But of course no rules are hard and fast. Red, like all colours, has variant levels, each of which can create very different moods. Shades like orange-red and brown-red (clearly much more muted than typical cherry red or berry tones) are very comforting, as are earth tones like cinnamon and brick red.

C&J'S TIP

Fashion should play a part in your choice of colours, so do some research on what the hot new colours are. Being informed will introduce you to a wider range of choices so you can ensure your home doesn't get stuck in a rut or end up looking like a museum. But don't become a fashion victim. Find your own style, get your key items in place, then add more or less colour, as required. Small changes from season to season will keep your home fresh and contemporary.

Yellow

Green

YELLOW IS A SHADE THAT TENDS TO CAUSE more eye fatigue than any other colour. In its sunniest tones, it can increase metabolism and is said to upset babies—which is why we tend to avoid using it in nurseries. Colour research has shown that some people, when they are in yellow rooms, can lose their temper, but we like to think we know how to play this colour safely. Balance yellow with either white or black, and you can take this vibrant shade in two distinct directions. In fact, our yellow and white combo in John and Linda's boudoir is widely considered one of our most successful transformations ever! At the other end of the spectrum, however, we softened yellow with black in the home of Laura and James and the results, while controversial, were similarly spectacular. Although there are yellow detractors, there are many more who agree with us that this sunny shade makes people feel cheerful, energetic, and alive.

If you like yellow but remain scared of its brighter shades, think about spreading more buttery tones around your home. The range of yellows is huge, and of course some tones lend themselves better to decorating than others. Think, too, of golden yellows, ochres, and sandy tones to help familiarize yourself with a decorating palette we adore.

GREENS REPRESENT A WIDE RANGE OF natural colours and so they appeal to many homeowners. Like blue, the colour green tends to be calming and possesses relaxing tendencies.

For home decorating, regardless of the room, olive and sage green are generally winners as they have a lovely neutral character, and lighter shades of both are easy to live with for a long time. Each combines well with many other colours such as cream and soft yellow. Dark greens are favoured as traditional decorating shades (along with colours like burgundy and deep blue) and that's why you see these tones used frequently in libraries, gentlemen's clubs, and restaurants. Hazy yellow-greens (and darker muddy greens) are relatively unpopular whereas zesty lime greens can be *fabulous*. And take a tip from us—team forest greens with rich wood tones and the results will be amazing!

C&J'S TIP

Put together a colour mood so you can easily mix and match tones to discover which colours work well for you. Use the freely available paint swatches from DIY stores or the online decorating software available at many paint company websites. Once you've plotted your room's colour, create your dream look around this palette.

Case Study:
40-Year-Old Grannies

Problem: This is the bedroom of two very colourful characters—so why is it so grim? The DIY bed platform looks like an oil rig and the overall effect looks like a squat rather than a beautiful boudoir!

Solution: Our plan was to design a room with sculptural elements and colour, ideal for the creative pair who live here.

Before

Plus Points

* Attempts at DIY furniture-making show some flare—but only a little!
* Standard-size double bedroom

Minus Points

* Looks like a peace camp—but a very *un*-peaceful one at that!
* Dated fabrics
* Terrible bed

After

Effective use of colour was our holy grail. We painted a pair of bedside tables vivid glossy red. This makes them stand out, and the gloss highlights the carving on each piece. Use gloss finishes when you're sure your makeover piece has no imperfections. Sand areas of concern before you paint—gloss will highlight great features and bad!

We chose the wall colour to provide a cool mood but we balanced it with hot red to create a more liveable mix. By itself, the blue might have been too low-key but the red provides that magic ingredient that makes our design "pop."

Punctuate strong colours with white to provide relief and contrast. The white bed, linens, and woodwork are welcome relief from the blue and red, and serve to make this a slightly Union Jack–inspired colour scheme.

Add colour with floor rugs, bed throws, and cushions, though make sure you leave breathing space around each for contrast. Here the wooden floor frames the rug and the white bedding frames the cushions and the throw.

More colour can be added through accessories and lighting. Here red candle glasses and a modern red light fitting (not shown here) perfectly punctuate the blue.

Before

Case Study:
Not So Pretty in Pink

Problem: The colour of this room was all a bit wishy-washy with no real power or pop! And as for that "colourful" haunted armchair, is it better with or without the throw?

Solution: Design a modern family room that has style and impact.

Before

Plus Points

* *Ehm*… positive points… ah yes—there's a cat on the wall?

Minus Points

* Colours all melt into each other to create a really drab environment
* No focal point
* Dated everything

After

The window wall has been decorated with striped wallpaper hung horizontally to widen the appearance of the wall. A single wall of paper is a great way to add colour and personality without over-committing yourself in time or cash.

Use a large single piece of art to add vibrant drama and to create an instant focal point. Coloured soft furnishings can also decorate a room. Here, the sofa provides a punchy red that is dramatic and highly practical too!

When using similar colours, try to use contrasting textures to add character. In this room, a fluffy rug in a warm tone sits on a faux limestone floor—the colours are similar but the textures are completely different.

Orange

ORANGE IS WARM, WELCOMING, AND VITAL
and we *love love love* this exciting shade. In fact,
whenever we get the opportunity we set the
juice loose! Whether melon, Satsuma, or
mango, we can't help ourselves! Heck, we use
this colour *everywhere*! In kitchens, bedrooms,
and in dining rooms, we find this palette both
invigorating and uplifting.

C&J'S TIP
Balance orange with loads of white or you'll
feel like you're living in a giant tangerine!

Purple

OH BLIMEY—THE COLOUR OF KINGS!
Opulent, mysterious, and *seriously* spiritual. As
all colours do, this one runs a huge range of
registers, from eggplant and lavender to shades
of the precious stone amethyst. Saturated purple
is a hedonistic and rich choice that will provide a
dramatic punch of colour when required. We
love mauve and lilac, and while some decorators
might consider these a more feminine battery,
we disagree! In fact, we went wild in Frank's
house and created a grown-up man's domain
with just enough femininity to keep *everyone*
happy.

Pink

Black

PINK IS AN INTERESTING COLOUR BECAUSE IT still bears the cultural associations of femininity. However, take it from us—it's a fantastically relaxing shade that we reckon men are now happier to embrace. In fact, many British shirt manufacturers and retailers (most notably one that is actually called Pink) have noted a massive upturn in demand for pink shirts and ties! In some of their stores, pink actually outsells white and blue alternatives!

But let's get back to the relaxing connotations of pink. Research shows that pink-painted rooms can reduce angry behaviour (at least while subjects are contained therein), which has led some prisons to select pink in their attempts to control aggressive inmates.

Great for young princess bedrooms (though as previously described, girls tend to be "over it" by the onset of teenage years), it's often a difficult colour to work with so we use it only occasionally. That said, we used it in this living room and kitchen combo. We're especially proud of these two rooms. Interestingly, the addition of steel in this gorgeous kitchen softens the look of the specially manufactured pink cabinetry while the addition of gold in the living room pulls out added—and almost regal— drama in our marshmallow scheme!

AS YOUTHS, WE BOTH HAD BLACK-PAINTED bedrooms, much to the chagrin of our parents. And we mean *all* black! Walls, bedding, carpets, the lot! Indeed Marilyn Manson, had he been chart-bound in those days, would have felt very at home. These days, however, we realize the power of restraint. Played out properly (as an accent wall, perhaps, teamed with taupe and white accessories), black can look seriously classy and sophisticated. Often better employed as an upholstery choice (we have black deep-buttoned chesterfields in our Glasgow home office), it can be butch but at the same time a little bit bitch, if teamed with mirrored furniture and sparkling crystal-encrusted accessories.

C&J'S TIP

Never choose colour based on small sections of a paint chart—always use the largest paint "chips" your supplier provides or paint large sections of card with your chosen palette. This makes it easy to try the colour in different areas so you can observe how the tone "behaves" close to a window in natural light or farther back into the room where illumination is more limited. Leave the painted card on a focal point zone—such as a mantelpiece—for several days and let the colour "surprise" you when you enter the room.

Case Study:
Pleather, Plastic, and Panthers

Problem: Does anyone actually live here? Talk about feeling bare—empty shelves and a lack of colour make this a real dead zone.

Solution: Create a living room with a young night-club feel for a couple of young funky homeowners.

Before

Plus Points

* Small but with potential
* Sound structural condition

Minus Points

* Two small rooms that need the connecting wall removed
* Pleather furniture

After

Think about using furniture to add colour to your rooms. The sectional sofa provides a splash of colour as well as adequate seating. The coffee and occasional tables add drama, while the black glass and mirrored accessories illuminate the entire proceedings.

Wallpaper appears in one colour on a feature wall at the back of the room and then again on three canvases in the same pattern but in a different colour. Who says you can't mix and match?

The colour combination used here isn't one for shrinking violets—you have to be pretty bold to appreciate this, but fortunately that's exactly what our homeowners were! When you see a great room on TV, in a book, or in a magazine and think, "Wow, that's the one for me," make a mood board on which you can display and try out paint samples and fabric swatches to see how it all feels. Live with it all for a few days and if you still love it, go for it!

Vases of fresh flowers are another great way of adding colour—just make sure you change the water regularly or your colourful table feature will become a smelly nuisance!

Before

Grey

GREY TENDS TO ENHANCE CREATIVITY, WHICH makes it a sensible choice for offices and studios, but we also use it regularly in other rooms. Selected as a soft "whisper" variation, grey provides a low-key background for an infinite number of colour combinations. Used alongside mushroom or brown tones, grey is traditionally softened and can help elicit either a traditional or modern feel according to the furnishing and other elements chosen. Add shots of baby blue and all of a sudden you'll find yourself creating contemporary, even beach house–inspired decor. Our own Toronto condo is bathed in sunlight so we've gone overboard and created an elegant, almost 1940s Hollywood feel. In fact, so happy are we with grey as a decorating dictum that it's a regular choice during our *Home Heist* adventures!

Brown

BROWN IS ALL ABOUT SAFETY, SECURITY, AND credibility. It's a soothing tone as long as you don't go overboard. If you do, your schemes run the risk of feeling a tad gloomy. From an economic perspective, browns wear well and are good for zones where heavy traffic is likely. It's crucial, however, to add accent tones. Cornflower blue is particularly good as a balance to brown, as are lime, light green, or, of course, cream. It's also worth noting that browns work well with spicy or warm colours such as orange and vibrant yellows. Just make sure there's good natural light if you plan to pursue this colour route.

Check out this kitchen to see what happens when you mix grey with black, crystal, and silver. In this *Home Heist* project, we deliberately kept to grey and white (with no accent tones), whereas in the living room, to soften the mood, we added wood finishes to provide elegant balance.

C&J'S
Top 6 Ways to Add Colour

1 **Paint One Wall.** Accent walls *rule!* And, what's more, confident blocks of colour can really change the focal point of your rooms without major decorating upheaval. Understand "restraint" because less, darlings, is generally more!

2 **Pitch in the Pillows.** Add pillows, throws, and accessories for drama in an otherwise muted scheme. Doing this will create decorating ease in the future as you'll be able to alter the room's mood on a whim by replacing old accessories with new!

3 **Add a Bit of Mother Nature.** Green plants or flowers will add visual warmth and personality. If you're not particularly green-fingered, ask your local garden centre to recommend horticulture that requires minimal care. Just *please* don't use fake plants. That is *such* a C&J no-no!

4 **Put Some Colour on the Floor.** A colourful rug, strategically placed in front of a chair or under your bed, will add colour and texture. Choose a contrast colour, inspired by fabric you're using elsewhere, or look for something with an interesting pattern that ties into your theme.

5 **Freshen up a Chair Cushion.** If you have a small chair, such as a desk stool or side chair, bring it back to life by re-covering it. Fresh colour on just a small area like this will help invigorate even the most tired scheme.

6 **Get Arty.** A colourful and strategically placed piece of art won't only add a decorative touch, it will also introduce drama and fun. It could be that the only thing standing between you and a vibrant scheme is a fabulous painting or some brightly matted and framed prints.

Paint and Paper

IF YOU'D SUGGESTED (EVEN TO PROFESSIONAL PAINTERS AND DECORATORS) as recently as twenty years back that the market would explode in the way it has, they'd have thought you bonkers. Even in the 1980s, wall covering choices were much more limited than today. If you wanted matte, satin, or gloss paint, you were pretty well catered for, but today's vast spectrum was merely a twinkle in product designers' eyes. Wallpaper choices, too, have grown massively and today's collections seem never-ending.

Although we love the great range available and the creative methods of applying paint and wallpaper, today's choices can be overwhelming. It's more than just deciding on a colour scheme these days. Getting "the bones" of your plan right is absolutely critical. When someone talks about the bones, it generally refers to the structure, services, and build and being sure the quality of these is top-notch before going any further. However, when it comes to decor, getting the bones right means creating a good decorative backdrop for other aspects of your scheme such as flooring, furnishing, and accessories. There's little point in barging ahead with these subsequent layers if you haven't set a good decorative scene.

Getting Started

ALLOCATE AS MUCH TIME AS YOU POSSIBLY can to working out the finer details of your scheme. It's far better to invest hours deciding which paper and paint you really like than days painting over or steaming off a purchase you've chosen in a rush only to regret it the minute it's on the wall.

We've found the following memory aid extremely helpful:

P C B G

P stands for **plan**: Decide what you want to achieve in mood, layout, and overall look.

C stands for **colour scheme**: Work on your tonal palette as a backbone for your new design.

B stands for **big items**: Depending on which room you're creating, choose beds, sofas, tables, etc. at this stage.

G stands for **gradual layering**: Accomplish this via accessories, artwork, and finishing detail.

Changing the look of walls will generally have a more dramatic effect than other design elements on your home's overall appearance so it's crucial that you tackle this stage thoughtfully. The great news is that doing so is fairly easy and relatively cost effective. Always remember that good preparation is critical and that rushed jobs will come back to haunt you. When it comes to good design—take it slowly!

Paint Options

FOR FEAR OF SENDING YOU TO SLEEP (!) WE'LL dodge the science lesson about the chemical composition of paint, and we'll veer, if you don't mind, toward basic description. Paint, essentially, is a combination of pigment (colour) and a binding product that allows it to be applied, evenly, to pretty much any surface.

In the past, oil-based paint was considered to be best at standing the passage of time, but manufacturing techniques have developed to allow today's water-based latex—and even acrylic—options to be just as effective. They usually dry faster and, all things considered, are more environmentally sound.

Here are the types of paint you'll find at your local paint-supply store.

Undercoat (also known as primer or base coat): Whether you're painting wood, drywall, metal, or brick, there's an undercoat product to suit your job. An undercoat provides a base to help subsequent paint layers adhere and also mutes the colour below. We know it's tempting to cut corners but, unless the paint you're using is specially designed as an all-in-one product (no primer required), then cheating will create poor results. *Fact*—preparing surfaces by cleaning and sanding provides a better surface for the undercoat and ultimately the top coat.

Regular acrylic: This type of paint is great for wee jobs around the house and for painting small details such as door knobs or trim. Because regular acrylic is water-based, brushes and rollers can be cleaned under your faucet.

Latex: In Britain we call this paint "emulsion" but whatever you call it, it's the optimum product for wall coverage. Available in every conceivable colour, this convenient water-based medium will wash out easily from brushes and rollers.

Oil-based: These products are, as their name suggests, oil-based. They're long-lasting but, as far as we're concerned (with latex paint now so improved), there's little need for them in this day and age. What's more, they tend to be more pungent than other paints and you'll need special paint thinner and brush cleaners to tidy up after each job.

Tinned spray paints: Spray paints are generally oil-based and are available in a limited, off-the-shelf range of colours. They are relatively easy to use and don't need the same level of preparation as brush-applied paint. They are usually used for small jobs or tricky items such as slatted furniture or pieces with lots of carved decorations.

C&J'S TIP

Always select the best-quality paint you can afford. Top-end products apply more easily, have better coverage, and, in our experience, last much longer.

Paint Finishes

IN THE WORLD OF PAINT, THERE'S EVEN MORE terminology that at first might be confusing. Never mind—here's the C&J easy guide to finishes!

Flat: This paint gives a perfect no-sheen finish (most commonly associated with latex) that is great on walls. A particular bonus is that this paint will help disguise surface imperfections.

Eggshell: Most commonly found in latex paints, this finish has a slightly more discernible sheen than flat but it still provides a relatively sheen-free finish. Particularly good where high traffic is expected as it's easier to wipe clean.

Satin: This is a great choice for bathrooms, kitchens, and kids' rooms due to its low-sheen, wipe-clean nature.

Semi-Gloss: Not quite at the top level of shininess, this paint is particularly good for trim, doors, windows, painted furniture, etc. as it's so easy to maintain. However, we recommend that you take extra care with preparation as the shiny finish will highlight any bumps or other surface imperfections.

Gloss: Need we say more? A dated finish that we tend to avoid. Period.

C&J'S
Top 10 Painting Tips

1 Preparation is key—sand, sand, and sand again...

2 Keep shiny finishes for smooth surfaces as reflected light will exacerbate any problems. Opt for matte or flat finishes if you're trying to disguise bumpy areas.

3 Don't be shy to ask a million and one questions in the store before investing in your paint. The staff are trained to assist you!

4 Never choose colour from a tiny paint chip. Many manufacturers now offer larger sheets of paint samples but we recommend that you buy a tester pot and paint a large patch, then observe it under different lighting conditions to see how it looks by day and by night.

5 Invest in good-quality brushes. If you buy cheap, you'll buy twice. And bristle loss will drive you to distraction!

6 Several light, even coats (with adequate drying time between each) are always better than one sticky heavy coat.

7 When painting wood, let your brush follow the grain to achieve best results.

8 Use small foam rollers on wooden surfaces and reserve larger rollers for walls.

9 Use the relevant cleaners and thinners (or simply water) as directed on the back of your paint tin. If you don't, you'll ruin brushes and rollers for the next time.

10 Remember to store some touch-up paint in airtight containers, and write the room and date on them for future reference.

Wallpaper

WALLPAPER, WHILE A MORE DIFFICULT CHOICE than paint, is an astoundingly good medium for adding drama and personality—and there are so many choices that it's mind-blowing. Before making your final choice, however, we recommend considering all the various wallpaper types to analyze which one is best for your job.

Lining Paper: This "undercoat" paper comes in various gauges and can be an effective way to even out surfaces when walls are bumpy. The thicker the lining paper, the more problems it will cover. It is designed to be painted or papered over with your final wallpaper.

Vinyl and vinyl-backed papers: Choose these for kitchens and bathrooms as they're both washable and water-resistant.

Paintable plain wallpaper: This option comes in a large variety of imprinted textures and is great for covering rough walls or surfaces with imperfections. When applied, it can be left as is or painted to suit your scheme.

Foils: These shiny papers will help reflect light around your space. They come in a wide variety of choices from retro to modern. Due to their construction, they're often water-resistant but, as always, check product specification before buying.

Flocked wallpaper: Approach these patterned lovelies with a degree of caution. Although they're interesting, they are also subject to fashion flux and are also harder to clean. Put them in low-traffic areas where they'll attract less dust. When we use these papers, we tend to limit their applications to focus zones or accent walls. Pick out a background colour (or a softer tone thereof) for other walls.

Woodchip: Beware—these are torture to remove further down the line! They are very dated and really only good to cover especially irregular surfaces. Our advice? Give woodchip a miss and prep your walls instead!

Relief: This type of wallpaper is press-printed with a raised pattern and is available in loads of different designs. Some have their own colour scheme and others are designed to be painted. Fairly easy to hang and, like woodchip, will help disguise surface imperfections due to their raised nature.

C&J'S
Top 10 Wallpaper Tips

1 "Think *twice*, buy *once*" was never more relevant! Head to your local supplier and, if possible, sign out some pattern books. Get them home to see how each paper looks in situ.

2 Get tooled up! Assemble sharp cutting scissors, a plumb "drop cord," a good pasting table, a large brush, and sponges to wipe down after each length of paper has been hung.

3 From our experience, small floral designs—while they're often very sweet—date more quickly so exercise caution when choosing these.

4 Be careful with larger designs and motifs—these are best used in generous spaces. Bigger repeats tend to shrink smaller spaces even further.

5 Stripe strife! Many rooms aren't completely "square" and, therefore, striped paper may not line up perfectly with doors and trim. Use a spirit level to see just how square your room actually is and adjust paper application accordingly.

6 For hallways and high-traffic zones, opt for patterned washable wallpaper to help disguise fingerprints and scuffs.

7 Try to find "paste the wall" papers. As the name suggests, adhesive is applied directly to the surface you're covering as opposed to the paper. Cuts out *a lot* of work!

8 Rub a lightly dampened sponge across paper as you hang it to remove adhesive buildup that will detract from finished results.

9 To ensure you don't run out, overbuy wallpaper with prior agreement that you can return unopened rolls.

10 Always buy paper with the same batch number to ensure shading is identical throughout your project.

Lighting

GOOD LIGHTING WILL EITHER MAKE OR BREAK YOUR SCHEME— it's just as important as your choice of colour or furniture. Used creatively, it can highlight features, make a style statement, and of course allow you to see after dark! And if you think that last point sounds obvious, you wouldn't believe the number of homes we've seen where we thought we were visiting mole people ...

Lighting falls into four basic functions: general, task, accent, and decorative. Each should be prioritized and attended to either on its own or combined to create a lighting plan that's controllable, comfortable, and functional. It's actually very simple ... just ask yourself, "What will I need and what form of lighting will deliver that?"

General Lighting

THIS BASIC FORM OF LIGHTING, ALSO KNOWN as ambient lighting, replaces natural sunlight in the hours of darkness and allows you to see clearly indoors. We like to make sure it's controllable so we can vary how much or how little there is. This form of illumination can be achieved through ceiling or wall-mounted fixtures, table and floor lamps, chandeliers, and recessed or track lighting and from a combination of task, accent, and decorative lighting.

Task Lighting

HAVING THE BEST LIGHT FOR EACH JOB IS what task lighting is all about. Assess what you do in each room (reading, cooking, working at the computer, doing paperwork, etc.) and provide good light for each task. Desk lamps, ceiling pendant fixtures, and appliance lights are all good examples of task lighting fixtures.

Decorative Lighting

THIS IS WHERE FORM AND FUNCTION combine! Or, in other words, when the physical lamp is as important as the light it emits! Examples include Tiffany lamps, which provide an eclectic air; Arco lamps and others like them, which create a feeling of modernity; lava lamps, which scream 1960s; or the out-and-out indulgence of chandeliers, which pump up the glamour factor to the max.

Starting from Scratch

IF YOU'RE LUCKY ENOUGH TO BE RENOVATING from scratch, plan where your sockets will be installed at the same time as all the "dirty" work is being done. Careful planning at this stage will ensure the lighting fits your needs and you won't have to trail unsightly cables everywhere.

And how about this for an idea! Isn't it great when you're staying in a posh hotel and you can switch on all the table lamps from a single wall switch? Installing this kind of set-up is *really* easy and will add the luxury factor, *especially* if fitted in conjunction with dimmer switches. And don't be scared to ask your electrician for advice—they, after all, have all the electrical answers. Chuck and Hugh, our *Home Heist* sparks, told us about remote-control dimmer switches and we've been obsessed ever since.

Accent Lighting

USE ACCENT LIGHTING FOR DRAMA, TO PICK out architectural features, or to highlight decorative elements like artwork and sculpture. This type of lighting should be employed in conjunction with general lighting to enhance overall mood. Floodlights, spotlights, track lights, and sconces are great ways to introduce accent lighting as their directional ability lets you highlight and draw attention where you need it most.

C&J'S TIP

Try to avoid direct lighting and favour diffused lighting instead as there's nothing worse than trying to work with a glaring bulb in your face. Add dimmer switches wherever possible for the greatest control over brightness.

Use Light to Problem-Solve

PROPERLY USED, LIGHTING CAN CHANGE mood, transform a boring box into an architecturally significant space, or cozy up a grand space. You just have to know where to use it …

Down Lighting

Down lighting brings illumination from overhead to mimic the natural down lighting properties of daylight. A pendant lamp is a classic general down light.
Advantage: Sure to reach all areas of the room
Disadvantage: Can cause ugly shadows on the face and look a bit harsh on its own

Up Lighting

Up lighting can be used to highlight architectural detail or to celebrate a feature you'd like to make more of—a lamp behind a plant or a fancy illuminated plinth with a piece of sculpture.
Advantage: Great for making more out of whatever you want to light up
Disadvantage: Can cause strange shadows on walls

Wall Washers

These types of lights can be either surface mounted to direct light up or down (up will push ceiling heights higher, down will cozy things up) or they can be ceiling mounted to illuminate one particular area.
Advantage: Reduce glare as light is bounced back into the room to create gentle ambiance
Disadvantage: Need to be properly balanced with other light sources or they can look stilted

Recessed or Pot Lighting

These popular types of lighting ensure that light is flush with the ceiling to provide all the illumination needed without taking up ceiling height. Low-wattage halogen lamps, which are frequently used in these lights, are both economical and pure in the light they provide.
Advantage: Modern, clean, and relatively inexpensive—a good all-round buy
Disadvantage: Cavity above the ceiling must be deep enough to accommodate the fitting

Spotlighting

Spotlights use a focused beam of light to highlight detail, artwork, or anything you want to make more of. They are available as surface track—mounted on the ceiling—or recessed.
Advantage: Can really celebrate a design by making more of key components
Disadvantage: Can cause glare and shadows

Lighting the Way Room by Room

Hallway

Your hallway is more than just a passageway to other areas. If you treat it like a proper room, the dividends will be well worth it. Remember, it's the very first impression visitors get of your home.

A well-lit hallway helps people to see where they should hang their coats or to find their boots when they're leaving. But flexible lighting in the hallway can provide the opportunity for mood setting. Fortunately, practical can be beautiful too, so install a swanky pendant, a lovely lantern-style lamp, or even a chandelier. Each is guaranteed to make a style statement as well as provide illumination.

C&J'S TIP

A table lamp on a console will create a cozy welcoming atmosphere. Or try highlighting a worthy hallway and staircase with floor-level lighting. Ask your electrician to install floor-level recessed spots to pick out interesting detail.

Living Room

Lighting a living room requires lots of thinking as you need to satisfy *so* many requirements. Why is it, then, that so many of the homes we see rely on one single pendant or a couple of lonely table lamps to light the way? Perhaps it seems too overwhelming—but it needn't be!

Let your lifestyle dictate your home style! List all the moods and practicalities you need from your space—subtle, cozy lighting for TV viewing and cuddling up in the evenings; overhead lighting for the kids to play; or task table lamps to allow you to read. Learn to create attractive vignettes by placing a pair of decorative lamps on either side of a credenza or by flanking a sofa

C&J'S TIP

If your ceiling is low, stick to flush halogen spots to "push" the ceiling height higher.

with occasional tables and lamps. If you're having trouble getting the ideas flowing, start looking at decorating magazines or visiting showrooms in furniture stores.

Dining Room

The focal point of any dining experience is the table, so it's well worth concentrating your lighting efforts here. Think "practical and beautiful" and remember how important mood setting is! And remember that electric lighting isn't the only answer … there's little more romantic than a candle-lit dinner!

When hanging a pendant shade over your dining table, make sure that it's low enough to create an intimate pool of light, but *without* glaring into the eyes of each diner. A lamp that is too low will mean diners are unable to look at each other during dinner.

C&J'S TIP

To get it right, sit down at the table and have your electrician adjust height as required—about 2 feet above the table generally works best. A dimmer switch is essential here as your dining room may also be used for other functions—kids' homework, for example.

Kitchen

Here, lighting must be practical and flexible—with the emphasis being on task. Mood should also pay a part as you might have an open-concept kitchen and will (we hope!) want it to look great even when not in use. Use overhead lamps to flood the space with light and remember to incorporate under-cabinet lighting to illuminate work surfaces. This is particularly important in food-preparation areas, as the glow from one single pendant lamp is not enough to work safely and your body shadow will create a dangerously dark chopping area. In short, good lighting will help avoid accidents.

You can easily fit under-cabinet lighting in an existing kitchen. A smart exhaust hood will generally include a lighting element to brighten up your cook top. Try to avoid fabric-covered lighting options as these absorb grease and smells. Also, keep lamps off the counter space to free up your work area. Make more of glass-doored cabinets by installing internal down lights to showcase china or smart accessories.

Bedroom

In this room you'll potentially require ambient lighting for dressing and making the bed, bedside lamps for reading, and maybe the odd lamp next to a chair. To free up bedside space, we've successfully hung ceiling pendants long and low on either side of the bed. Also try hanging wall lamps above the bed, hotel style.

Whatever you choose, make sure (as always) that it's dimmable and that you can operate it as you enter the room *and* from the bed. You can now get remote-control wall switches that can be operated from any part of the room—attention to detail such as this will really turn your room from ordinary to extraordinary in a flash.

Home Office

Desk work needs task lighting, so make sure your work station is well lit—a good desk lamp should be perfectly adequate. If you're short on desk space, an adjustable floor lamp will do the job equally well. If you have a computer, avoid glare from lamps by using diffused shades to provide even illumination and to make sure light doesn't bounce off your screen. You may need extra lighting near your filing cabinet, printer, scanner, or other office necessities if they are located some distance from your desk.

C&J'S
Top 7 Lighting Tips

1 Add a twenty dollar dimmer switch to create flexible mood control at the twist of a button.

2 Don't expect an overhead centre pendant light to provide sufficient illumination—the best-lit rooms are those that are served by a combo of overhead and side lighting.

3 Hallways look wonderful when dressed with long, slim console tables propped, either end, with attractive lamps that complement overall decor. Position a mirror between them to bounce light even further.

4 Don't think the high street is your only shopping solution! The online lighting market has grown massively over the last few years, so run a Google search using terms such as "table lamp," "overhead light shade," or "standard lamp" for a host of bright ideas.

5 To create atmospheric lighting pools, position discreet lamps behind sofas and chairs, but ensure that fabrics don't get too near light bulbs to avoid heat build up and fire risk.

6 Under-cabinet kitchen lighting (this falls into the "task" category) is a great way to provide extra illumination when preparing food, but also looks great as mood lighting at night when overhead options are switched off.

7 In rooms with low ceilings, keep pendant fixtures OUT and pot lights IN! Opt for dangle-free slick pot lights or ceiling tracks that don't interfere with sight lines.

Flooring

CHOOSING THE BEST AND MOST APPROPRIATE FLOORING CAN BE A DAUNTING task as it's such a huge commitment in terms of design and expense. But what's going to be underfoot is worth serious deliberation to analyze whether your choice ties in with your overall design or to help you narrow down the overwhelming choices. In short, you want to know—is it right for the job?

Form and Function

FIRST THINGS FIRST: THINK ABOUT THE LOOK you hope to create. Will those Moroccan glazed tiles, for example, really work on a kid's bedroom floor? Next, think about utility—will your guest ensuite really benefit from wall-to-wall carpet? Once you've assessed the relationship between form and function, you're well on your way to discovering the best flooring for your situation.

Upkeep and attractiveness are not mutually exclusive concepts, so choose floor coverings for pleasure as well as practicality—because surely you want to *love* your finished room as well as simply use it, *n'est-ce pas?* And if you're planning to buy a heavily patterned carpet, make sure your intentions are honourable! Do you *really* like that patterned Berber or are you just planning its installation because you believe it will hide dirt and stains? Remember—we know you, we've been to your home …

Suitability

FUNCTION AND SUITABILITY ALSO GO HAND IN hand when it comes to flooring. In a bathroom or kitchen, for example, you'll need a floor covering that's easy to clean and resistant to water and other spills. In your hallway or in kids' rooms, you'll want a friendly, durable option that can withstand heavy traffic. Perhaps you're a bit of a sex kitten and like nothing better than padding around barefoot in your bedroom, so choose comfy soft carpeting to up the tootsie-tickling factor.

Always consider how much traffic the room gets, whether you want your floor to add a particular colour or texture, to lighten up or darken space, and whether the type of underfloor you're laying it on is suitable to take what you have in mind. Suspended wooden floors, for example, are not an ideal base for tiles because of shifting and movement, and if you lay lino directly on top of tile you'll probably end up seeing grout lines as the lino settles. If you have any doubt at all, quiz your flooring contractor or ask in your local big-box store for guidance. And don't be shy to take some digi-snaps to the store so you can accurately discuss plans. Good staff, after all, have the expertise and knowledge you're after so don't be scared to go on an information harvest!

C&J'S TIP

Safety first—make sure your flooring choices don't present any danger. For example, a highly polished tiled floor will become an ice rink when wet shoes are added to the mix. If you're using rugs on hardwood or tile, you *must* use a rug-gripping underlay to avoid slips. Unless, of course, you're practising to become a member of the Canadian National Curling Team!

Noise

FLOORING NOISE (OR PREFERABLY LACK OF) is an important factor, especially in condos and apartments. Harder options like ceramic, stone, marble, quarry tile, and wood can all reflect and magnify sounds, whereas carpet, cork, rubber, and vinyl offer good sound absorbency. You can use underlay and specialist insulation to deaden sounds but it's worth noting that some floors will cause noise problems in the rooms below.

C&J'S TIP

Condo boards have strict guidelines about which products can and can't be used, and they're likely to have a rating system (based on decibel levels) for different floors. So check first (before buying) to avoid the hassle of store returns.

Role of Flooring in Design

FLOORING CAN BE A GREAT WAY TO UNITE adjoining rooms for a seamless and unified design. That's why we generally use one floor treatment of the same finish throughout the projects we work on. This means we usually specify wood or carpeting, which can easily move from the hallway to the living room to the dining room. However, if we have to change product in the kitchen or bathroom, we'll tie everything together with colour. This makes all the rooms feel larger and provides continuity from zone to zone.

Extra Costs

THERE'S MORE TO COSTING FLOORING THAN just the price of the wood or tiling or carpeting. You also need to take into account how much your flooring will cost to fit. Will you have to remove and plane down internal doors? Do you need to lay a self-levelling substance before work starts? Will you need to line your existing floor with plywood before laying carpet? All these things will affect the project's cost and should be taken into account when budgeting.

C&J'S TIP

Apply a little future-proofing to your plans: think of introducing or maintaining easy access to pipe work and electrical elements—the last thing you want to do is have to remove your recently tiled or hardwood floor when an emergency crops up.

Flooring Guide

HAVING TROUBLE DECIDING WHAT TO PUT underfoot? Here's an overview of some new and not-so-new options.

Carpet

Soft and warm underfoot—perfect for bedrooms, living rooms, and low-traffic hallways, and relatively easy to maintain. Carpet comes in many forms such as smooth cut pile, textured frieze, level loop (like Berbers), and multi-level loop patterned. It also comes in many fabric types such as nylon, polyester, and wool, as well as options such as coir, seagrass, and jute. It's worth buying the best you can afford but don't be afraid to get the look of more expensive options with a wool/man-made fibre mix. Best installed by pros as specialist tools and stretchers are required.

Laminate

Hard-wearing and good for hallways, living rooms, and bedrooms. Designed to echo the look of real hardwood, this cost-effective choice can be durable and easy to maintain. Some manufacturers claim that this type of flooring is stain- and warp-resistant although the cheaper options, from our experience, tend to swell up in the joins when exposed to moisture. Often the choice of the DIY installer, but we'd caution that budget flooring can look cheap if badly installed.

Solid Hardwood

One of our favourite flooring mediums as it's beautiful, warm underfoot, and durable. This choice can be used all around the house as long as it's properly sealed. We recommend, however, being extra careful to guard against spills (especially in bathrooms) as wood can warp. The denser the wood genus (ask your supplier for info), however, the safer you'll be. Available in strip, plank, or parquet form, and endless colours of stain, hardwood can be resurfaced and resealed many times.

Engineered Flooring

Essentially a thick veneer of real wood laid on a composite board, this option provides great flexibility and can be used anywhere. It is particularly popular in condos thanks to its good sound insulation. It's a practical option that graces the floor of our own Canadian home!

Vinyl Flooring

This all-round flooring is great throughout the home, especially as it's now available in so many different colours and finishes. Resistant to both traffic and moisture, it's an oldie but a goodie! But boy—has it changed! No longer just that small roll of monochrome tile-effect plastic in your local DIY store, today's sophisticated easy-care vinyl floors come in plank, tile, or roll form and can offer as much as a twenty-five-year guarantee. Its low profile also means that, nine times out of ten, you won't have to remove your internal doors to accommodate the thickness of the floor.

Tile Flooring

Depending on climate, tiling can be great anywhere in the home, though some consider it

C&J'S TIP

When applying special floor paints, don't cheat to try to speed up the application. Follow the manufacturer's instructions and remember that several light coats are always better than one gloopy application. If you don't want to invest in a dedicated floor paint, you can use standard gloss or satin and protect it with a couple of layers of clear varnish.

cold and unwelcoming. We, however, like to celebrate the good points! It's easy to maintain and relatively cheap to install, the range available is absolutely breathtaking, and there's generally a cheaper "get the look" version of any expensive tile you can find. A must for the bathroom! But if you use it elsewhere, you can warm it up with scatter rugs (held in place by good-quality no-slip undermats).

Tiling includes ceramics and marble, but if you're looking at heavier stones, be warned that there may be areas where it's not possible to lay such weighty flooring. If you're concerned, we'd always recommend seeking professional advice before installation. The "stress" weight of a stone or ceramic floor in a large area such as a living room can easily approach a tonne—imagine that weight spread across beams that might be undermined by age or poor condition. In such a situation, reinforcement or an alternative product may be required.

Bamboo Flooring

Made with strips of split bamboo laminated onto plywood planks, this floor is robust and resistant and good for use everywhere—especially in bathrooms, due to its waterproof nature. It's worth spending a little more on a really good-quality option as some of the cheaper varieties can splinter. And good news! Where the environment is concerned, this flooring solution is *fabulous!* Because it's made from fast-growing and sustainable bamboo grass, it's a clear winner as a renewable resource.

Cork

Also a renewable resource, cork flooring is great for all-round home use. Some manufacturers claim it is especially good in bathrooms due to its natural ability to resist mildew growth. Great also for soundproofing and insulation between floors. We love its quirky retro pedigree and plan using it more and more on *Home Heist!*

C&J'S
Top 6 Flooring Tips

1 Stay on the level—there's nothing worse than a trip-hazard step up between rooms. And, wherever possible, use the same flooring between open concept rooms to visually enlarge space.

2 Be practical—if you're a hyper-minimalist with a home that looks like an art gallery, then perhaps a white floor will be perfect for you. If, however, you have four kids, three dogs, and a gecko, then maybe not! And remember that carpet in the washroom or bathroom is a no-no …

3 Use your choice of flooring as decor and make sure it adds to your overall design—funky white polished tiles, for example, wouldn't exactly complement a "gentleman's club" brown leather sofa, whereas a hardwood floor would look perfect.

4 Think of toe comfort—you want things to feel wonderful underfoot so invest in under-tile heating if your kitchen's a bit on the chilly side!

5 Don't go overboard with pattern—a floor is a huge investment, so opt for a simple design and change the mood with rugs.

6 Use flooring choices to lighten or darken your room as required. Think TWICE, buy ONCE, and imagine how your new floor will look as part of the bigger picture. Don't buy anything in isolation—every "layer" should add to and complement your home's overall design.

Accessories

AHH, *ACCESSORIES!* AS FAR AS WE'RE CONCERNED, IT'S THE COLLECTIVE TERM FOR GORGEOUS wee decorative nuggets. Those flavoursome little cubes should simply burst with identity to complement your overall design. Actually, come to think of it, we prefer to call them "successories" because, used properly, they'll successfully complete your room!

Here's the deal: Let other TV "experts" tell you that accessories are simply clutter, but let *us* assure you differently. Carefully selected accessories are *not* clutter. Clutter happens when there are too many things dotted around your space that don't share a common relationship. Put simply—good accessorizing should add to overall harmony, it should reflect your taste, and it should be made up exclusively of things that matter.

The Power of Accessories

TO APPRECIATE WHAT ACCESSORIES CAN DO FOR a room, imagine a bare, basic holiday home or cottage. Sure, it's furnished—with sofa, tables, beds, and so forth—and it's probably equipped with a stove, a vacuum cleaner, and a TV, for instance, but without accessories to finish it off it looks cold and impersonal. Then imagine a gorgeous hotel room with great objects in the bathrooms, interesting artwork on the walls, and vases filled with fresh flowers. The former is dull, the latter is nice—that's all there is to it. Carefully selected finishing touches will ensure hotel guests feel welcome—and better yet, indulged—unlike the other folk who checked into the depressing guest house. *That's* the power of the accessory …

Choosing Accessories

SO JUST HOW DO YOU PICK ACCESSORIES that are right for the job? Being properly informed is the starting point, and using that information to help bring your rooms to life is the next step. Let's consider an example. Perhaps you're keen on all things Asian, and maybe you have a rattan sofa and rustic wooden coffee table. Both are great starting points for your preferred look but to pull it all together you need to research Asian style just a little more. Consider some of the aspects that make it successful—wood tones, natural finishes, religious symbolism, etc.—and then go shopping, remembering it's not how much you spend, but how you spend it that counts!

Don't be afraid to experiment when you've created the bones of your look. Huge slabs of stainless steel and chrome won't exactly complement your Asian dream, but it's still fun to leave scope for an element of surprise, something that stops your room from being a carbon copy of every other Asian-inspired room. A great example of this kind of thinking would be adding an intricate antique gold-framed "Old Master" in a modern loft apartment. Sure, it's kinda out of character, but it could be kinda funky at the same time …

Accessories and Decor

Whatever the style, accessories should be compatible with your overall decorative scheme and they should—for the most part—relate to your colour palette and the room's overall mood. When we're dressing a project home, we tend to begin with the owner's choice of books and art, as these are usually extremely personal and provide great clues as to individual style. Family photos are important, but displaying them is just as important—try to unify your display by framing and matting each in a similar style. Or consider new methods of image display such as pictures printed as pop art canvases. Or use digital art frames to move through your family or holiday pictures automatically. One frame, multiple rotation! It's the minimalist's dream …

Quantity is also worth considering—we know that less can most definitely be more, so invest in a smaller number of larger, significant pieces rather than a muddle of little bits and bobs. This tactic won't only look better, it'll also save you time, because quality over quantity means fewer items … less work!

Picture Hanging

PICTURES SHOULD BE HUNG SO THE MIDDLE of the image is approximately at eye level. The magic number is 56 inches, measured from the centre of the piece to the floor. This is the perfect height for the average person in the five-foot-eight to five-foot-ten range. Some designers tend to float their artwork much, much higher but take it from us—following this guideline will provide for far more comfortable viewing. Think about it—when was the last time you went to an art gallery and had to crane your neck to appreciate the display? *Precisely.*

Soft Accessories

IN BEDROOM PROJECTS, WE ALWAYS SPECIFY loads of comfy cushions to add a splash of colour and texture, and in the living room the same principle applies. You'll find that carefully selected throw pillows will punch character into your scheme and enliven even the humblest sofa. But don't stop there—layer on some tactile throws and watch the drama build!

Grouping Accessories

TRY TO GROUP ITEMS THAT VARY IN HEIGHT from tall and medium through small. A good example of this is a bedside table dressed with a lamp, a picture frame, and a small ceramic. Or perhaps a dining room credenza dressed with a tall mirror, a medium-sized sculpture, and a dainty ceramic bowl. Experiment with various items until your look comes together.

C&J'S TIP

Designers generally like to position accessories in groups of threes or fives, and while the science part of this tactic baffles even us, we recognize that odd numbers simply look best!

C&J'S
7 Favourite Accessories

1 Artwork
Artwork is the perfect way to add colour and drama while spelling out style. If you want to add identity but feel wallpaper is too big a step, then add a (changeable) canvas or print.

2 Rugs
A good rug will do for a floor what a piece of art will do for a wall—it'll add colour, style, and identity. Rugs are also an ideal way to map out open-concept rooms and delineate dining from living zones.

3 Mirrors
Mirrors are a great way to make spaces feel larger and brighter. A mirror above a fireplace or a credenza will look fabulous, while a mismatched cluster on the wall adds immediate eclectic personality.

4 Vases
We love to fill vases with fresh blooms, just DON'T be tempted to use fake flowers—it's worth doing an "Elton" and splashing out on the real thing!

5 Family photos
We like displaying family pics, but cluttered surfaces strewn with mismatched frames leaves us cold. Create uniformity by selecting complementary frames and visually connecting pics with matching mount cards.

6 Lighting
Considered floor and table lamp selection will bring identity *and* illumination to your space. Just make sure every addition complements your overall design.

7 Textiles
Switch up mood with soft furnishings—cushions, scatter pillows, and textural throws add colour and drama that can be seasonally adjusted.

Notes

Notes

Notes

Notes